PRAISE FOR CONF

Jason Digges has dedicated his life to helping us humans relate to one another more authentically and compassionately. This book represents a lifetime of study, practice, and teaching, useful for both students and practitioners... a practical, wise, user-friendly collection of best practices. This is an important and much-needed book for helping people join together in creating systems and communities where we help one another heal. You know the old saying, "It takes a village." Jason's new book shows us how.

— **Susan Campbell,** Ph.D. Author of *Getting Real, Saying What's Real, Truth in Dating,* and *Five-Minute Relationship Repair.*

Inauthentic relating lives at the heart of so many of the world's issues. Too many reactive assumptions, too few genuine inquiries. In this visionary book, Jason Digges hands us the tools we need to humanize and enhearten our relationships. His brilliant offering is a sacred blueprint for individual and collective transformation. I recommend it highly!

— **Jeff Brown,** Author of *Grounded Spirituality* and *An Uncommon Bond.*

Jason Digges has a profound, passionate practice in bettering human relationships. His personal work, his immersion in authentic relating, and commitment to community has resulted in this volume. If you take it to heart, it will provide real guidance to anyone who wants to deepen and enhance their relational lives.

— **Diane Hamiton,** Author of *Everything is Workable* and *The Zen of You and Me.*

Finally, a wise and eminently practical guidebook to authentic relating and circling. Jason Digges has concisely encapsulated the important principles and key practices of this rich world in a way you'll be able to understand and actually implement.

> — **Terry Patten,** Author of *A New Republic of the Heart*
> and *Integral Life Practice.*

In a world of so much polarization and misunderstanding, each of us needs to learn to be honest and vulnerable. That's easy to say, but harder to live. This book is the A to Z guide to living in wide open tenderness.

> — **Arjuna Ardagh,** Author of *Radical Brilliance*
> and eleven other books.

Did we really think we were doomed to be social media automatons? No, a new consciousness is arising, what Jason Digges calls the Human Connection Movement. Central to it is the practice of Authentic Relating, the fruits of which Digges transmits in this wise and beautifully-pitched book. He provides both the map and means, through a series of well-honed practices, for growing into nothing less than the next stage of human relations, for both individuals and the culture at large.

> — **Jeff Salzman,** *The Daily Evolver Podcast.*

CONFLICT
= ENERGY

The Transformative Practice
of Authentic Relating

For more information, address:
conflictequalsenergy@gmail.com

First paperback edition July 2020

Cover Design & Art Direction by *Ash Witham*
Interior design by *Ruslan Nabiev*

ISBN 978-1-7350760-0-3 (paperback)
ISBN 978-1-7350760-1-0 (pdf)
ISBN 978-1-7350760-2-7 (ebook)

www.AuthRev.com

Authentic
Revolution

Pass the torch
Pass the light
Pass the warmth
Pass it to someone you care about
Pass it to someone you don't care about
And should you find yourself lost in the dark
Come find me

—SAMSON LEE

TABLE OF CONTENTS

Foreword
STRATEGIC AND HONEST COMMUNICATION

We all live in a private world: of thoughts, evaluations, fear, emotions, fantasies. Most of what you experience, no one will ever know. It is uniquely yours. *Does he like me? There's not enough money. Oh my god, I can't believe I just said that. I'm such an idiot. She's looking at me, quick, smile! Act friendly!* We send missives to each other across the great chasm of our mental and emotional isolation.

Most communication ends up being strategic, designed to cause the other person to feel and behave in a certain way that fulfills our agenda. Although we may understand that communicating strategically is not the way we want to live, it is modeled to us so frequently that it just winds up becoming our default.

More or less all marketing is strategic. It is designed to make you feel desirous of something you don't have, or to make you feel inadequate in some way about your appearance, or your wealth or your status, with the agenda that you will then give your money to the entity that created the advertising.

Politics, particularly in the U.S., is entirely strategic. Politicians can be bought in various ways, by corporate donors, or just by the immediate needs and desires of their electorate. In order to get into office, you have to be popular, and therefore you need to "launch a campaign" in order to make people like you.

Sadly, a lot of educational institutions are also strategic, feeding the aspiring student along a conveyor belt of prepackaged knowledge. Each and every step is designed to help you meet another goal, pass another exam, and move on through the process to eventually become an obedient cog in the socio-economic machine.

The media, which long, long ago, in a land we can hardly remember, was designed as a vehicle of honesty to counteract all these forces, has also become, just within our lifetime, highly strategic, competing for the short attention span of its readership. The media has become expert at sensationalist headlines, page-turning copy, often fueled by fear to whip you up into a frenzy, and then win you as a loyal repeat customer.

Flirting and seduction are strategic, whether done with words, body language, or the selective display of naked skin. When we flirt, it may not actually be with the deliberate intention to end up in a relationship or in bed, but instead, it carries the agenda of wanting reassurance that I'm attractive and that you love me.

In fact, any kind of attempt to control anybody with rules or guidelines or suggestions or "feedback," is strategic. It's designed to have another person conform to my idea of what I think is the best way to live, and therefore to create a feeling of being in control. Any form of harassment or intimidation is strategic. It's designed to generate a feeling of fear in the other person, so they back down and allow you to get your way. The ultimate expression of controlling behavior is of course violence.

Because almost everything we are fed systemically smacks of strategic communication, many of us have come to regard this as normal in our personal lives as well. As a result, too few of us have role models for rich, nourishing, truthful relationships.

Strategic communication is not just about overtly lying. We are also being strategic when we withhold relevant information, which the other person would actually like to know. Having a secret affair, secret porn watching or gambling all require withholding, but not always lying.

The antidote to strategic communication is called being "authentic." It's strange, isn't it, that just over the course of a few decades, authenticity has become something we have to deliberately practice. It has become the exception, rather than the norm. Most of us need a strong reminder now and then about why honesty is a good idea. This book offers you the simple tools to restore simple honest authentic communication to your life.

Authentic communication is the opposite of strategic. It does not guarantee you to make more money, have more power, to quickly get more love and approval, or to have more sex. It simply returns you and the other to a state of innocence.

Authentic communication is always a risk. You can easily be rejected if you are honest, you can be laughed at if you do not support someone else's narrative and agenda. You also risk not getting what you think you want, and sacrificing your own agenda at the altar of innocence.

What is innocence? It's ineffable. It's a lightness in the chest. It's laughter for no reason. It's a feeling of unconditional safety, not because of external circumstances, but because a weight is lifted from your heart. Innocence is an innate knowing of your own essential goodness and that of the other.

None of this comes easily or automatically. It requires a courageous commitment, each and every day, to swim against the current. It requires us to splash cold water on our faces, to put aside the habits of strategic communication, and to take a stand for being yourself again, a return to innocence.

This little book that you hold in your hands by my buddy Jason Digges is not another academic tome from an expert. It is a joyous invitation from a courageous friend inviting you back into the sandpit to play, and to rediscover the lightness of being that has always been yours.

Arjuna Ardagh
Author of *Radical Brilliance* and eleven other books

July 14, 2020
Nevada City, CA

ACKNOWLEDGMENTS

The curriculum of Authentic Relating is the result of over a decade of many leaders' living, breathing, and inspiring this material. These and other powerful practitioners and contributors have built the Circling and Authentic Relating (AR) movement into what it is today. The roots of this book are in the collaborative effort of several pioneers advancing a vision of new possibilities in human relating. Each of them has significantly contributed to my thinking, and my acknowledgment of them goes far beyond a simple "thank you." Together, we have laughed, we have cried, and we have birthed this practice into an emerging global phenomenon.

Sara Ness, founder of Authentic Revolution
Laurie Lazar, executive director of ARI Nonprofit
Decker Cunov, founder of Authentic World
Robert MacNaughton, founder of The Integral Center
Michael Porcelli, Josh Levin, and Jess Nichol, the early leaders of the T3 Courses

You hold in your hands a synthesized and concise guide to Authentic Relating. The full spectrum of its teachings lives in the oral tradition of thousands of practitioners and hundreds of leaders all over the world. As we enter an age of transparency in 2020 and beyond, I believe innovative ways to heal disconnection in our society will increasingly be shared as open-source wisdom.

And now, my personal invitation to you is to take the practice, the tools, and the skills from this book, and adapt and apply them as they suit you.

Preface

THE QUEST OF CONNECTION

I've always been a crusader. Growing up in a family of preachers and missionaries, some of my most cherished moments as a child were being curled up in a blanket while the adults played acoustic guitar and sang songs about Jesus. The church offered me purpose, community, support, and a place to grow.

As I grew into a young man, I began a quest reaching beyond the church that sought to integrate the Christ-inspired message of universal love with common experiences that all humans could share (Christian or not). I began a meditation practice and dove into my own soul, studying psychology and various personal growth methodologies. In these early years, I gained some peace of mind, and some insight into what truly makes us tick as human beings—but life was largely still painful and confusing. I was especially challenged by how people treated each other during conflict—including myself!

Then in 2011, I discovered a relational practice called Circling, and that's when my life's purpose truly began to take shape. Circling is a practice of being here and now. It brings us into deeper relationship with each other, with ourselves, and with the magic and aliveness contained in the present moment. Circling is also quite practical, and improves our relationship and communication skills by helping us see ourselves more clearly. As we will explore in depth throughout this book, the experience of becoming more in touch with ourselves and others in tandem is the key to accelerated growth.

Within one year of discovering this practice, my identity shifted rapidly. I went from a place of painful social anxiety to one of stepping into leadership. In all of the seeking I'd done the decade previous, I'd never experienced personal transformation like this. In Circling, and later, Authentic Relating, I witnessed people making leaps in their personal growth, becoming aware of lifelong patterns, clarifying their needs and desires, and learning how to express them.

By 2015, I was traveling across the world to participate in courses and community events, from Boulder to New York, from Amsterdam to Austin. I was determined to get in touch with the pulse of what has since become known as the Human Connection Movement—a movement that has taken many forms and seen many teachers. By this time, Authentic Relating "games" were spreading across the globe, and the practice of Circling was becoming more defined, with some leaders also creating experimental new forms. It was an exciting time. My friends and colleagues were growing like crazy—transforming! So was I, and I began to wonder, "What are the core elements that are facilitating this growth?"

As someone who'd grown up in the church, I realized what was (thankfully) missing from this new movement: divisive dogma. Practices like Circling, Authentic Relating, and other connection tools that were growing in popularity during this time didn't require me to believe in anything—and yet, they provided that same glowing warmth I'd experienced in the church in my younger years.

A new question began to drive my quest: "Can humanity find a narrative that unifies us?" Many of the things that gave us meaning and a sense of identity in the past, like religion, class structures, or gender roles, can also cause division or even violence and war. Can we come together around a shared story? I believe the answer is yes, and I believe this story will celebrate our differences instead of fueling emotional and physical violence through dogma.

As I kept exploring this question over the next five years, I stepped further into leadership in the budding movement, facilitating hundreds of groups around the globe in seminars and workshops. Throughout all the travel and searching, I was asking myself what this new human narrative of unity would be. Slowly, a vision began to take shape in my mind.

If we could train enough people in the essential connection skills of Authentic Relating, and also teach people how to navigate conflict in their relationships, then we could create unity out of the profound differences among us.

Conflict in our relationships is scary and painful for all of us. And yet, it holds the key to a thriving life, because our differences provide energy for psychological and emotional growth. Our closest relationships are the most fertile place for building emotional maturity, and the growth of the individual is, I believe, the way to transform society.

Peace is not the absence of conflict
but the ability to cope with it.

—GANDHI

Fifteen years into this quest, I have now compiled everything I've learned into this book, which aims to both illuminate the essence of these powerful practices, and also be a practical guide for us to transform our relational lives. You now hold a synthesis of teachings and tools for this body of work that my colleagues and I call Authentic Relating.

Put simply, Authentic Relating, or "AR," is a set of communication practices designed to bring us into deeper connection with one another, with ourselves, and with the world around us. I believe it is how we'll grow our circle of care and compassion. My hope and vision is for a society that can learn to be inclusive of the people around us, seeing people not as "others" but as part of one unified tribe—because we must. As our population and connection technologies expand, our world gets smaller and the problems we face grow more complex. Therefore, our hearts must grow bigger.

If we can just count more people as part of our circle of care, if we can only realize that connection is simple and as necessary for our survival as food, and if we can remember that connection is free and available with anyone, despite our differences, then maybe, just maybe, we can leave behind the divisions of dogma once and for all.

As I write this, the Earth's population is approaching 8 billion people. That's a lot. I wonder how many of us can truly grasp what a number that high means for our society and planet.

I wonder if we can all find ways to thrive together.

With love and radical acceptance,
Jason Digges

PART I
AUTHENTIC RELATING:
Theory and Practice

An Overconnected World

We are living through a loneliness epidemic, one whose size and scope could never have been predicted before the telecommunications revolution. Genuine conversation and learning to build nourishing, lasting connections are more important than ever. This is partly because of the ubiquitous presence of technology, device and screen addiction, and partly because our value systems are changing so rapidly. Meanwhile, relating to each other remains the most foundational aspect of society, and AR aims to cultivate intelligent and clear education for our emotional and social lives.

Of course, feeling lonely is part of the human experience. If we are to embrace the full range of our emotions, then we must accept that loneliness is just one of many flavors that makes life rich. Feeling consistent loneliness and a chronic lack of emotional nourishment, however, can degrade our quality of life. Taken to its extremes, "social starvation" can cause depression and other negative psychological and physical health challenges. Just like a baby needs touch and eye contact to develop, adults need social and emotional connections to thrive. Neurobiology shows us these are genuine, physical needs.

A 2018 study showed that three in four Americans feel lonely consistently.[1] In the UK, research identified 9 million citizens suffering from loneliness to the point of severe mental and physical health issues—so much so that the country appointed its first-ever Minister for Loneliness.[2] Another study from the Harvard School of Human Development took a 75-year-long look at the elements that lead to a fulfilling human life. This is the longest study on the topic ever conducted by Western scholars, and shows a direct and strong correlation between the quality of one's relationships and fulfillment at the end of one's life.[3]

What we are learning from the science is a commonsense conclusion. Put simply, long-term wellbeing and other qualities of a thriving life depend in large part on the quality of our closest relationships.

This adds up to a very strange picture. The populations of the most-developed countries in the world, with more access to each other than ever before in human history, are the most

1 Lee, Ellen E., et al. "High Prevalence and Adverse Health Effects of Loneliness in Community-Dwelling Adults across the Lifespan: Role of Wisdom as a Protective Factor." *International Psychogeriatrics*, vol. 31, no. 10, 2018, pp. 1447–1462., doi:10.1017/s1041610218002120.

2 *Trapped in a Bubble*. Co-Op and British Red Cross, 2006, *Trapped in a Bubble*, www.co-operative.coop/campaigning/loneliness.

3 Vaillant, George E. *Triumphs of Experience: the Men of the Harvard Grant Study*. The Belknap Press of Harvard University Press, 2015.

depressed. To grapple with this phenomenon, we must understand that personal-level mental health challenges live within a much larger societal-level context.

When we examine the population of the world today in light of globalization, the picture becomes clearer. Fifty years ago, the human population of planet Earth was 3.6 billion. Today, we're at nearly 7.8 billion. That's over double the number of people drawing on the same amount of resources, and that number is only increasing. We are surviving with the same amount of precious metals and clean water, and the same amount of physical land and space in this biosphere. And while our technologies and population have grown, has our capacity for sharing and caring also grown proportionately? Human society has evolved in so many complex ways, but have most of us even truly learned those earliest childhood lessons about sharing, cooperating, and being kind and fair to each other?

Human technology is both a blessing and a curse. Despite being more connected than ever, the populations of many wealthy countries are struggling to *feel* connected. As we will see, this is vital for creating the sort of thriving communities that empower the emotional and mental health of the individuals within them. What we need more than the latest smartphone model are reliable skills to regulate our own nervous systems, so that we can bring more energy and emotional resources to our work and to those close to us. Feeling connected and a sense of belonging to the tribe sets us up for thriving and fulfillment—as individuals and as a society.

Why Authentic Relating?

Authentic Relating provides us a detailed emotional curriculum that can be practiced between members of any community or group (from couples and friends, to companies or parties in conflict or mediation). The curriculum in this book includes practices for advanced listening, honing our intuition, and creating acceptance of our full selves. We will also explore how to cultivate dignity and humility, a key to living an authentic life. These tools can help us grow our fundamental relationship skills with surprising speed, ultimately benefiting our personal, social, and professional lives.

But it doesn't end with us as individuals. The work of opening our hearts and cultivating emotional intelligence benefits the planet and humanity as a whole. We *must* learn to navigate conflict and tension with dignity and humility in this rapidly-changing world, so that we can survive and thrive as a species.

Authentic Relating plays a significant role in this survival by offering a sustainable way for individuals to improve mental health. In coming decades, as we grapple with complex factors in a globalized society, AR may also come to play a vital role in social health, an emerging field of research into factors that help communities thrive.

The Authentic Relating skill set has been developed over many years, by many different teachers. These teachers are from varied backgrounds, but have in common the desire to understand human development. We have run countless circles, thousands of "games nights," and hundreds of immersive multi-day workshops. When we as leaders compare notes, one thing becomes clear: Empathy and emotional resilience are learnable skills.

Through these practices, people around the world have experienced a beautiful range of changes: recovering from social anxiety, developing more confidence, learning how to better handle their emotions in tense situations, expanding creativity, transforming work, friend, and family cultures, and becoming more collaborative with others! Of course, these results take dedicated practice, but Authentic Relating can work remarkably quickly.

Most importantly, these skills can also form the basis for humans to work together to devise solutions to the most pressing problems we face as a species. With education in these vital areas for many, just imagine the benefits this could have on a global scale!

How to Use This Book

The intended audience for this book is broad, ranging from those brand new to Authentic Relating or personal development work, to experienced AR practitioners. We'll begin with the simplest foundational teachings, and gradually progress to more nuanced concepts and immediately applicable skills. In Part I, we explore the theory and practice of AR, and what living and communicating authentically with those around us can look like. In Part II, we'll discuss the pedagogy of AR, and the most potent tools for creating emotional intelligence within individuals and cultivating social health. Finally, Part III looks at how to transform conflict and tension into abundant and productive energy.

Dispersed throughout the book, you will also notice a collection of "Power Tools," which aim to synthesize pieces of AR wisdom into tools that can translate easily into your everyday life.

Chapter 1
POLARITY

Conflict is really what sharpens our ability to Love.

—John Gottman

Which is better, day or night? Which would you choose to have all the time? If you're a little confused, you're on the right track. These questions make little sense, because the phases of night and day are drastically different. Night and day are polar opposites, yet equally essential to life as we know it.

Light and dark, cold and hot, stillness and movement... Life on this planet is the way it is because of these polarities. To ask you to choose which is better is tantamount to asking you to choose a different universe altogether! By definition, neither pole would exist without the other, and we as humans could not exist without them both.

How about deciding between compassion or truth? Or authenticity and belonging? Again, there can be no clear "best" answer here. Yet as humans, we are asked to choose and prioritize values all the time—and we certainly have judgments about other people's values! These judgments are a main source of our tension with each other. Embracing polarity can help us be more open to considering the values of those around us, even when we don't agree with those values, let alone understand or appreciate them.

Wrestling with polarity, paradox, and nuance is essential to human life—for us to coexist and thrive together. We avoid developing this relational skill at our own peril, though it is admittedly difficult to manage that kind of emotional complexity.

We can think of a polarity as two interdependent concepts or values that seem in opposition at first glance, but truly balance and are at the heart of one another. The practice of Authentic Relating embraces both sides of any polarity. This is a fundamental element of the practice. Once we can learn the art of being able to hold or appreciate multiple perspectives, a tremendous amount of relational power and energy become available. The title of this book, *Conflict = Energy*, comes from this concept.

It is a sign of cognitive strength to be able to hold seemingly contradictory facts in one's mind at the same time. It is a sign of emotional strength to hold both sides of a disagreement with a loved one as valuable. And it is a sign of personal mastery to be able to stretch our minds and hearts to hold multiple perspectives in the face of conflict.

In practical terms, Authentic Relating teaches us to speak and hear uncomfortable truths without blowing up our relationships. In other words, we develop the skill of being our fullest, most authentic selves, while still respecting others—even when their beliefs and perspectives may differ. This ability to value both our own view, and the views of others, is a key that unlocks the door to a more fulfilling life.

Mastery of a skill set takes practice, and this crucial capacity to navigate polarity is no exception. This book shares practices and tools to help us incorporate the fundamentals of conscious communication into our lives, and charts a path for us to master these skills. Conflict is an opportunity. AR allows us to uncover the nature of that opportunity—to truly know ourselves and others by exploring the needs and values underneath our differing perspectives.

If we seek to better understand both our own values and those of others during the more challenging aspects of a relationship, we have the chance to harness the energy of conflicting perspectives. As we grow to cherish the experience of connection, clarity, and cooperation that are the fruits of truth-telling, we increasingly find the courage to bring our authentic truth forward. We come to learn that the payoff is worth the risk and effort, because through this approach, we get to be ourselves fully *and* be in close connection.

Navigating Conflict Using Polarity

Next time a conflict arises in your life, practice the following:

- Pause.
- Slow down.
- Start to ask questions, such as:
  - "How might both of us be correct here?"
  - "What is beyond right and wrong in this situation?"
  - "How can I integrate these two perspectives into something that takes into account both of our values?"
  - "Can I stay open to this person even if I don't like what is happening?"

- "Can I stay connected to my perspective without using it to attack another person's?"

The reason many of us are poor at handling our conflicts is that it requires us, in a sense, to go against thousands of years of evolution. We are neurobiologically wired to protect ourselves against threat or loss. When we feel our emotional territory is threatened, we tend to react, and usually with strong emotions.

We may "shut down" our empathy, get defensive, or even preemptively attack.

Short, exploratory questions like the sample questions suggested above can help us skillfully navigate conflict. Instead of putting our attention into defending ourselves, the practice of AR teaches us to respond by looking at our own somatic (bodily) cues. As we ask these types of questions, and we notice what happens in our body, emotions and thoughts, more space is created inside of us.

The simple practice of *noticing* is fundamental to Authentic Relating. When we practice getting in touch with our bodies in moments of conflict or stress, we become more somatically grounded and embodied. The word "embodied" literally means "including the body." It is so central to AR that it will be our focus in the next chapter.

Remember, *conflict equals energy*. When there are differences, it only means there is more juice to work with—more energy to move us toward our goals in life. Harnessing this energy of polarity is where the practice of Authentic Relating can begin to really open up.

AR POWER TOOL
Can We Slow Down?

This simple question is one of the most important tools in the AR toolbox, especially when tense moments arise in our close relationships. Under stress, our nervous systems tend to reactively speed up: a natural response to fear or threat. This adrenal activation, sometimes described as an "adrenaline spike" or "being triggered," primes reactive (and potentially harmful) responses. This is why slowing down is such an essential tool in AR. Doing so gives us time to explore possibilities beyond our automatic conditioning.

Authentic Relating doesn't necessarily heal those places that cause unhelpful communication and relationship patterns: That would be the realm of counseling and psychotherapy. But in a potentially more elegant and often much quicker way, AR simply puts new options on the relational menu.

A state of being activated or triggered is also when our generosity and compassion for others can be at their lowest. Sometimes both people in a situation may be interacting from an activated nervous system. In cases like this, we are very likely to see some fireworks—and not the good kind!

In tense conversations, simply slowing down and taking a few breaths or asking a few collaborative questions can work wonders. Try these open-hearted questions the next time you find yourself in conflict:

Can we slow down?

Can we sit down and give this the attention it deserves?

I need to slow down. Would you be willing to take a few breaths with me?

Avoid saying things like:
You need to slow down.
Calm down!
You should take some time to cool off.

These latter statements are laced with control dynamics that can further inflame the current conflict. On the other hand, "Can we slow down?" invites collaboration and shared accountability.

Dignity and Humility

> *My perspective and yours*
> *Two directions life will use*
> *steering us towards truth*

One of the most important polarities we work with in AR is that between *dignity* and *humility*. Dignity is the quiet strength and presence that comes when we have access to our voice and our truth, and can speak these freely. Humility is the receptivity and grace that comes from knowing that we always have something to learn from others. Both are necessary components of the wisdom we admire in many leaders.

Is Bishop Desmond Tutu dignified or humble? How about Gandhi? Or Thich Nhat Hanh? In truth, it's not one or the other. Leaders capable of creating peace and unity wherever they go deeply embody the qualities of both dignity and humility.

To remain dignified in a conflict means that, no matter how open and receptive we are to another, our own inner compass and voice are not suppressed. To embody humility in a conflict is to acknowledge that, even if we believe we are right, our view of the situation is partial. Since one of the goals of Authentic Relating is to train ourselves to mastery in holding both sides of this polarity, we need to develop awareness and skills in each, and appreciate both deeply.

When looking at a specific polarity, we must also examine the shadow expression of each side. When used in this book, the term "shadow" means the information that we choose to hide, suppress, or deny—those parts of ourselves that Carl Jung described as our unconscious aspects. As Jung said, "The less the shadow is embodied in the individual's conscious life, the blacker and denser it is."[4]

The shadow qualities of dignity and humility are posturing and collapsing, respectively. These are primary defense mechanisms we employ to handle fear or threat of any kind. We either expand or contract. We either posture to make ourselves seem bigger, or we collapse and negate ourselves in some way.

Posturing might look like becoming rigid to protect our sense of self. We puff up to intimidate others by becoming

---

4   Jung, Carl G., and Richard Francis Carrington Hull. *Psychology and Religion, West and East.* Routledge & Kegan Paul, 1958.

aloof or untouchable. On the whole, this defense mechanism leaves others feeling like we are inauthentic or untrustworthy. But when we pause to feel this defensiveness in ourselves or others, we can't help but also sense the insecurity underneath.

Collapsing might look like making ourselves smaller or suppressing our voice, as a strategy to avoid making waves with others. An inner voice quietly insists, "Don't rock the boat!" so we collapse in small ways and acquiesce to others. Collapsing and discounting ourselves is a tactic that can become so habitual, we cease to even notice it.

Waking up to all the patterns of posture and collapse we play out with the people in our lives can be quite humbling. The truth is that we all do this. We all experience adversity, we all feel fear, and as a result, sometimes we posture. In other moments, we collapse by saying nothing or apologizing. These patterns exist to hide our vulnerability.

Ironically, this is *exactly* the perfect starting point for being authentic! Authenticity means including all parts of ourselves, even the ones that hide our insecurities. Each time we reveal a part of us that we would normally put a mask over, we take a big step toward living a more authentic life. The shadow points the way to the gift. By recognizing patterns of posture and collapse, we teach ourselves to be more dignified and humble, and this is essential for leading an authentic life.

By practicing this polarity, we may even be able to stretch our inclusivity toward the other eight billion humans out there. Fortunately, we don't need to lose our dignity to do so. In fact, it's essential that we don't.

Authentic Relating as a Polarity

Our authentic expression is a powerful force, but one sometimes seemingly at odds with the sensitivity required to be in relationship with others. Think of a two-year-old authentically expressing himself through a temper tantrum; it can be overwhelming to witness so much intense energy channeled through such a small body. Now imagine an adult (weighing five to ten times as much as that two-year-old) behaving in a similar way. Any wonder or compassion you might have had for the toddler would likely be replaced with fear or anger.

Tantrums are a type of posturing, and these selfish emotional displays are damaging for adults. Adults who can't control their anger often find themselves making a mess of their relationships, yet this massive energy is precisely part of what we're trying to harness with AR. If enough of us can learn to channel our emotions into direct, peaceful action and communication, we can ultimately form thriving and healthy communities.

Of course, we can't just go around saying everything that comes into our minds! Sharing our authentic truth is done in relation to other people. We must take into account both authenticity *and* respect for the other people involved. We speak our truth with respect, and then we check in with others and "get their world" (explore their perspectives) about how what we shared was received.

Forgetting either side of this self/group polarity can get us into trouble. Our ability to balance the two will have a direct impact on the level of fulfilling connection in our relationships, and therefore the overall health of our communities.

Chapter 2
EMBODIMENT

Knowledge is just a rumor until it lives in the muscle.

—Saying from Papua New Guinea

In many ways, this book is a type of emotional resilience "fitness guide," filled with workouts and stretches to help strengthen and soften your heart and mind. Your physical tissues—all the bones, muscles, organs, and blood—are the territory of this journey, because they are so entwined with our hearts and minds. In some far out way, intelligence literally inhabits different parts of our physical form, and Authentic Relating reconnects us to our bodies and all of the important information stored there.

In our study of embodiment, we'll start by considering another polarity that can produce tremendous energy: that between *vision* and *embodiment*. We'll consider vision first, and then spend the bulk of this chapter understanding the nuances of embodiment.

Vision — Imagining a New World

Simply put, our vision is our imagination: whatever we can dream up with our ideas and creativity. This is the realm of insight and possibilities. To open our minds wide enough to embrace both sides of a polarity is a creative act. Stretching our ability to encompass multiple perspectives can generate new insights and possibilities—but we cannot see the benefit of these understandings until we learn to translate them into action.

We tend to lack trust for creative people who never produce anything from their ideas: those who seem to be all talk and no follow-through. Sometimes we may even feel as if such individuals lack substance, like they're not "all there." These people are "all vision and no embodiment." They have not mastered holding both sides of this particular polarity.

How might we avoid being one of these types? How do we create what we dream of and bring our ideas into the shared material world? We must learn to harness the energy of both vision *and* embodiment, by living in the *balance point* between the two. We'll circle back to this important concept of the balance point in a few pages. First, let's discuss the other half of this equation.

Embodiment – Creating a New World

When we are embodied, we are "here" in the present moment—more in touch with ourselves and more available to others. We are in tune with our surroundings, active and aware, yet relaxed and responsive as well. There are many ways to phrase this concept: "being grounded," "feeling ourselves 'in' our bodies," or "centered," to name a few. If you're familiar with the concept of being present, the definitions above probably sound quite familiar. But the question remains: How do we grow this sense of presence?

Of course, we're not always embodied. Anytime we slip into daydream, ruminating over an annoyance at a co-worker, or worry about the coming days, we are drifting away from our fully-embodied experience. While some downtime from full embodiment may be necessary for proper rest and integration, a lack of embodiment and grounded behaviors can have a negative impact on our relationships. If you've ever heard or said something like, "You aren't listening to me!" or, "He's just not *present* with me," that's a good indicator that, at least in that moment, a lack of embodiment was affecting the relationship.

Those who practice embodiment regularly have a certain solidness about them, and are more able to bring the full array of their intelligence to serve their desires. Becoming aware of our physical bodies, and the sensations that arise within, is the act of embodiment. And when we intentionally expand our embodiment skills, we grow our capacity to be present with our internal experience. This allows us to listen to others more deeply, pay attention more fully, and to offer those we're listening to more of ourselves in a supportive way.

While this may not come as a surprise, it's worth emphasizing that increasing our level of embodiment can have a massively positive impact during conflict. When we can transform intense emotions in a difficult conversation, by feeling them fully and stating them with calm acceptance, we increase our capacity for emotional resilience. Control of our nervous system grows each time we can remain constructive in our communication during a tense moment.

This skill is vital for good relationships. When we are embodied, we are better able to feel, sort through, and process our emotions via physical sensations. This ability to delay the gratification of immediate expression, in favor of the long-term gratification of effective action, is one important aspect of *emotional intelligence* (a phrase coined by the science journalist Daniel Goleman).[5] We will talk much more about the importance of emotional intelligence and resilience, and how to develop them, in Part II and III of this book.

The Balance Point

Now that we have a solid grasp on a few different polarities and their importance, let's talk about bringing them together in harmony. The balance point between vision and embodiment exists when we are connected to the sensations of this present moment, and to a possibility for the future, *at the same time.* This allows us to be in touch with our values here and now, while steering ourselves solidly toward the vision for our lives.

So, the balance point between vision and embodiment is what gives us the energy to turn our vision into a physical reality—or as the saying from Papua New Guinea goes, *Knowledge is just a rumor until it lives in the muscle.* When we embody something, we become it. Day by day, we become the vision we have for our lives when we live in this balance point.

---

5   Goleman, D. Emotional Intelligence: Why It Can Matter More than IQ. Bloomsbury.

As we flesh out a couple of other polarities throughout this book, we can get in touch with the abundant energy at the balance point of each one. Remember, in any polarity, these forces are always dynamically moving: You aren't going to find yourself at exactly 50 percent of each pole over time. Instead, a polarity fluctuates, and we can learn to surf those changes in energy.

The more we are attuned to our experience of the "here and now," the more energy we will have for manifesting our vision in the world. The more we can hold dignity and know our voice matters, the more we will also be able to hold humility and truly listen to others when they differ from us. The more we value our relationships and belonging, the more time and emotional energy we will devote to being authentically ourselves. This concept of "the more the more" is one worth remembering, to help us understand the value in both poles of a polarity.

AR POWER TOOL
The Body as Compass
or "Let Me Check"

In the tangle of all our conflicting needs and desires—and the expectations that the people we love may have of us—making decisions can sometimes feel impossible. In these situations, tuning into our thoughts can often confuse us further, as several voices within us may all speak up at once. But what if we really allowed ourselves to *feel*, trusting the compass of our *bodies* instead?

When we are asked to make decisions, we often answer automatically. The invitation here is to pause first and "check." In that pause, try imagining yourself on either side of the decision—noticing the sensations of your body as you do this. On one side, is there pain? A sense of weight or resistance? On another, is there an expansion, or a sense of aliveness or peace? If the sensations you feel are mixed or unclear, you can always say, *Let me get back to you.*

When we don't pause, or lack this trust in the guidance of our bodies, we can easily fill our lives up with "shoulds" and obligations. Answering others with, *Let me check*, and tuning in our sensations, is not only a form of honoring our own needs. It's also a practice of embodiment, and a means of sharpening our self-understanding.

Body Intelligence

There is an intelligence in our bodies that is far more vast than anything our conscious mind is capable of. One of the most marvelous things about this system is its ability to absorb and assimilate new information. A study into the unconscious processing abilities of the human brain estimates that roughly 11 million pieces of information per second are absorbed by the unconscious mind; this number is even more unbelievable when compared to the estimate for conscious processing speeds of around 40 pieces per second.[6] Yet even this astonishing statistic doesn't tell the whole story.

Each cell of our body is surrounded by a cell membrane that perceives the environment and determines what passes in and out at the molecular level. The profound intelligence of these cells can't be grasped by the conscious mind. It's a super-intelligence that lives in our bodies and speaks a different language. Yet by learning to be more embodied, we are learning to speak this language, and to bridge the innate intelligence of our bodies with the symbolic language that makes up our cognitive, conceptual self.

This universal translator of embodiment is the capacity to decipher our emotions and sensations into intelligent, "choiceful" actions. It allows our bodies, minds, and hearts to be in communication with each other, and the integration of all three is essential to the development of emotional intelligence.

---

6   Wilson, Timothy D. *Strangers to Ourselves: Discovering the Adaptive Unconscious.* Belknap, 2004.

Embodiment and Technology

As a last thought, let's consider the impact of technology on the general level of embodiment in the world today. Most of us don't even leave the house without our devices: miniature portals that transport our minds to someplace else. With mere flicks of our fingers, we have access to every stimulating piece of information offered on the Internet. We tap, swipe, and "like" our way through virtual worlds, while absorbing comments from dozens or hundreds of other people interacting with the same content.

By diving into the more mental world inside our phones, we easily lose touch with our more *embodied* experience. If we include laptops, tablets, televisions and department store displays, we see that individually and collectively, our minds are constantly engaged in what must truly be considered a virtual reality. When our engagement is assigned to something other than what is happening in the physical world around us, we more easily become disengaged from our senses.

It's little wonder, then, that so many of us struggle in relationships these days: We spend much of our time practicing disembodied behavior patterns! The drops of dopamine and emotional feedback we receive from the glow of our screens fill a function for social validation that would otherwise be met through embodied conversation. As a result, the ability to form deep connections in our human-to-human interactions may be stunted from our lack of use.

Traditional ways of improving our capacities for embodied living include: dance, yoga, sports, martial arts, etc. While these are a decent start, these activities aren't enough. With devices influencing more and more of our lives, we must all put in the time for embodiment through deliberate practice— and we must do this in our everyday actions and interactions. We need to slow down while in connection with others to reflect on what we are feeling, thinking, and wanting. We need to give ourselves the time to feel into our decisions and what is right for us individually, so that we may authentically embody what is right for us collectively.

The AR movement is at a critical tipping point: The world needs this work, perhaps now more than ever. As the influence of technology increases, being present to experience meaningful human connection is critical. Stay embodied. Stay human.

Chapter 3
THE FIVE PRACTICES
OF AUTHENTIC RELATING

Some people think they are in community, but they are only in proximity. True community requires commitment and openness. It is a willingness to extend yourself to encounter and know the other.

—David Spangler

Within the The Five Practices of Authentic Relating lies a comprehensive toolkit for an individual, community, or society to operate with a balance of love and truth, authenticity and compassion. These practices contain both a structure for how to direct our awareness, and the tools to grapple with the complexity of all that it means to be human.

With these tools, we can learn to live in the balance point between belonging and expression. This is a central polarity of Authentic Relating that acknowledges we need both: to feel the safety and support of connection, as well the freedom to express ourselves fully.

In short, these practices unlock the capacity to sustain empowered, alive, nourishing connections, and constitute a day-by-day and moment-by-moment map of how to build that capacity. They form the core of the Authentic Relating framework. They are:

- Welcome Everything
- Assume Nothing
- Reveal Your Experience
- Own Your Experience
- Honor Self and Other

Practice 1: Welcome Everything

Tension, conflict, and dissatisfaction are part of life. Rather than try to avoid or resist these inevitabilities, this first practice invites us to *Welcome Everything.* We greet with gratitude (or at least awareness) both our "positive" and "negative" experiences, and the full spectrum of emotions that comprise what it is to be human. Welcome Everything is the gateway practice to all the others. If we begin by welcoming every experience as meaningful in its own way, we can then get curious instead of pushing our experiences away.

The opposite of welcoming, of course, is rejection. The mind has many defense mechanisms it may engage to do this, but the two that we will discuss here are *repression* and *suppression,* because both are forms of inauthenticity. In the simplest of terms, to suppress an experience is to push down some natural expression or reaction to a person or an event, because it doesn't fit with what we think others will accept. This is driven by our biological need for group approval and, ultimately, survival. Suppression is usually driven by a fear of social consequences and of how we might be perceived.

Another main form of inauthenticity shows up when we hide things from ourselves and pretend we aren't aware of them, primarily out of fear of the intensity of those emotions. This is repression. Repression usually leads us to numb out or avoid our emotions in some way. Both suppression and repression are forms of rejecting and resisting our experience.

These two defense mechanisms are formed in childhood, are adaptive, and may even be healthy during those early years. In adults, however, they can keep us stuck in unhelpful patterns and prevent us from learning and growing. They also reduce our ability to be authentic. When we decide instead to *Welcome Everything* in our experience, we challenge these old habits.

Welcoming often feels like we are widening and "efforting" to expand ourselves to include more. It takes a lot of energy to behave in opposition to old patterns, especially at first. Yet the more we practice welcoming, the easier we find it—until it becomes a way of life. This brings us into harmony with life, because we are no longer resisting what is. Though it may take effort to cultivate this habit, we will find that it actually saves us energy in the long run.

In addition to our emotions and inner world, welcoming everything also includes the people and circumstances around us. Yet it must start from the inside, because this is the core of our sphere of influence. One of the great gifts of Authentic Relating is being able to receive others with acceptance for who and how they really are. It's not always easy, but the more we practice welcoming our own internal experience, the more we can bring this capacity into our relationships—and the easier we will find it to navigate life's challenges as a whole.

If, on the other hand, we choose to avoid things by sweeping them under the rug, they don't actually disappear. This colloquialism illustrates that realities persist, hidden in plain sight, lumped under the proverbial rug. Over the course of our emotional lives, repressed or suppressed experiences build up until they cause numbness, depression, anxiety, or other ailments. A much healthier, more effective way of processing is to turn *toward* our experiences, and deal with reality accordingly in the moment.

Notice the phrase, "deal with reality accordingly." The practice of welcoming everything does not mean *tolerating* everything, or putting up with physical or emotional harm. There are certain situations that we must not tolerate for the sake of our integrity and ethics—and others that we must strive to change, improve, or influence, simply because we care. Before we move into action, however, we must first allow ourselves to fully acknowledge those situations. In this practice, we allow our experience in, as if it were knocking at the door—even (and especially) those parts that are painful and hard to look at. Only when we face our internal experience in an honest way can we meet our external reality as it is.

The moment we practice welcoming everything, we can actually feel a change in our bodies. Resistance and repression have a certain feeling tone in the body, as does the attitude of welcoming. Many people report a relaxing of tension in their neck and back, a decrease in the pressure in their face and hands, and feelings of peace, joy, or clarity. As our mindset changes, our physical responses shift as well. This feedback loop of positivity becomes possible whenever we stop expending energy trying to control others, and instead allow it to flow back to us. While this is by no means easy, it can be remarkably powerful to embody.

AR POWER TOOL
Permission to Vent

Anger, resentment, frustration—difficult feelings like this can be destructive if bottled, but also toxic if mindlessly "dumped" on others. So how the heck do we "welcome" all the stormy emotions of life?

The key is in our awareness and intent. If we are willing to take responsibility for our emotions, we can actually enroll others to help metabolize our experiences. In this tool, we can give ourselves "permission to vent," through the practice of welcoming everything (as well as context-setting and consent—which we'll discuss in more depth later).

Far from irresponsible, *conscious* venting can be a radically mature and respectful act. We first find someone we trust, and get their buy-in to receive our energy; e.g., *I need to vent. Would you be willing to listen?*

This is a markedly different experience from gossip or complaining. We do not vent to put others down, or to raise ourselves up. In conscious venting, we are choosing to welcome the energy of our emotions, so that we can ultimately come to a place of more dignity and more humility.

When we express our emotions with conscious intent (rather than suppress or repress them), we become their director, rather than their puppet. And when we purposely bring others into the process with consent, we allow them into our vulnerability—instead of sucking them into our stories and dramas.

Practice 2: Assume Nothing

Tens of thousands of years ago, human nervous systems developed the capacity to catalogue, store, and communicate information about the world. This was an essential evolutionary upgrade, allowing us to apply past learning to current situations, and to visualize and predict possible outcomes in the future. We use this capacity to create safety and structure in our surroundings. After all, these things are essential for our survival.

Imagine the pressures our ancestors faced, constantly needing to ask themselves, *Will I die if I eat this? Will this person or animal hurt me? Will this action help me secure more resources?* Ultimately, these are all variations of the question, *Will I be safe?* We have evolved with this primary focus on survival, and as such, we tend to want to make our world predictable, especially when it comes to our most essential needs. These imperatives in our nervous system also process social tension as a kind of survival threat. In fact, current neuroscience research shows that our brains give us emotional pain signals when we deviate from group norms or detect disapproval from others.[7]

Our brains are constantly creating expectations and assumptions about our environment and the people around us, so that we might successfully anticipate and solve problems. This includes how to fit in socially. The human nervous system is simply designed this way; there's no getting around

---

7   Fisher, Nicole. "Emotional & Physical Pain Are Almost The Same - To Your Brain." *Forbes*, Forbes Magazine, 26 May 2020, www.forbes.com/sites/nicolefisher/2020/02/14/emotional--physical-pain-are-almost-the-sameto-your-brain/#2db030bb46c1.

it. And while it has been essential for our survival as a species, it can also wreak havoc in our relationships.

We have all kinds of past experiences stored in our brains and bodies at the subconscious level. Our subconscious mind is continuously and rapidly pattern-matching what is happening in the present moment with what has happened in the past. It does its best to predict what might happen in our future, and it does this for our own good. After all, responding to danger is easier when one is prepared for it!

The process is complex. Imagine that your subconscious mind is like a supercomputer. Right now, it is tracking an incomprehensible array of variables beyond your awareness of the screen in front of you. If something in the present moment seems similar to something that was perceived as dangerous in the past, our inner defenses will become activated. We may feel a little tense, or lose patience with others more quickly—all before we have any conscious awareness that something is happening for us emotionally.

At the outset of this emotionally triggered response, we have an opportunity. With some training, we can extend the amount of time during an "activation" that we are able to keep our higher brain functions within our conscious control. However, if we enter a fully "triggering" experience, all bets are off, and we can find ourselves acting in ways that sabotage or damage relationships.

This opportunity between stimulus and response is where we employ the practice of *Assume Nothing* to extend that time. This is a teaching beautifully illustrated in the anonymous quote: *Between stimulus and response there is a space. In that space is our power to choose our response. In our response lies our growth and our freedom.*

When we assume we know what's about to happen based on our past traumas and experiences, we rob the present moment of its mystery and unique expression. Often our assumptions are incorrect, and therefore our actions, attitudes, or communication is misattuned to the actual situation. Assume Nothing is a practice that births us into a place of curiosity and learning.

Of course, the practice is not as simple as learning to cease assumptions. As we've seen, our evolutionary impulse for safety has been with us for millions of years. So while we can't expect ourselves to simply stop having assumptions or expectations, we can mitigate the harm they cause. Here's how:

Step 1: Notice

This is often the hardest part. Asking ourselves to notice our assumptions or expectations is a bit like asking a fish to notice the water it's swimming in. Part of the reason it is so hard to change habitual responses is that they feel so natural to us.

So, the invitation is first to notice. Do you feel, for example, anger when holding onto certain thoughts? Or constriction around that big talk with your boss? What's the story you're telling yourself about what happened or might happen?

Simply notice these things, and then notice what it feels like in your body to drop your assumptions and expectations. As you do so, does anything else release? Do you feel more open? Excited? Sleepy? No matter the feelings, just continue to notice them. Over time, this simple act of noticing allows us more space before reacting.

Step 2: Get Curious

As we notice the feelings that come with our assumptions, we can begin to bring genuine curiosity to our experience with another. Try asking yourself questions like:

What am I assuming in this situation?

What is served by my holding onto this assumption?

How might this assumption be holding us back from openness and connection?

Step 3: Check Your Assumptions

Finally, check your assumptions about people by vocalizing them to the other(s). Be open enough to state what you perceive and what you are responding to; then, be open to feedback. Ask, for example:

I'm imagining that you want me to be _____.

Can you let me know if that's right?

It seems like you feel _____. Does that fit for you?

Can I check my assumption about something here?

When we practice these three steps, we move toward a life with fewer unchecked assumptions, and therefore, fewer relationship roadblocks. Remember, we will never be able to definitively rid ourselves of assumptions. We can, however, strive toward something better by consciously engaging our curiosity.

AR POWER TOOL
Is That True for You?

Since there's no getting around our assumption-making habit, playfully reframing our assumptions as guesses can be helpful. Sometimes we are right, sometimes we are wrong—and most times, we are actually somewhere in between. That is, our intuition may be picking up on something accurate, while we color in the rest of the picture with our biases and projections.

As we will explore in more depth in Chapter 7, adding a flavor of curiosity to our biases is a profoundly compassionate act. Curiosity simply desires to know the truth, and being wrong about our guesses is just as welcome as being right. From the perspective of Authentic Relating, we should consider being wrong a success!

Asking others to confirm our assumptions can be a massive source of information. Try stating your guess in simple language, and then follow it up with, *Is that true for you?* This short phrase offers the other person the space to articulate their reality, and we learn both more about who they are, and about our own patterns of assumption. These questions can also be a way of showing our respect, letting others know we care about them enough to endeavor to truly understand their perspective.

Practice 3: Reveal Your Experience

Once we have curiosity on our side, revealing what's under the surface of our interactions becomes more accessible. *Reveal Your Experience* is the phrase Authentic Relating uses to describe noticing a part of our experience, and being vulnerable enough to admit it—to ourselves and then to others. This means turning our attention inward, to determine our feelings, wants, and needs, before turning out attention outward, to share in the spirit of connection.

Only when we're willing to share what is going on inside ourselves can we truly begin to relate authentically with others. This is vitally important for connection: We cannot be known, felt, and seen by others if we don't reveal ourselves!

Feeling disconnected from those close to us is often a symptom that we're hiding some part of our experience. We can end up feeling resentful when we keep feelings or thoughts bottled up, which eventually can create breakdowns or disconnection in the relationship. We can only receive the nourishing experience of being known by others when we have the courage to reveal ourselves to them.

Sometimes, the reason we hold back from sharing ourselves more fully is the fear of being received poorly. Yet more often than not, revealing something that feels awkward or inconvenient is a service to others. This sort of conversational leadership often brings people closer. In fact, once you take the risk of revealing your experience honestly, you might hear responses from others like, "Thank you for saying something! I was feeling that too, but didn't know how to share it!"

Even if something we reveal is received poorly, we are usually doing right for the relationship in the long run (as long as our intentions in sharing are sincere). Regardless of the outcome, this practice does require embracing discomfort. Over time, we learn to trust that if we can muster the courage to say the uncomfortable thing, our efforts will ultimately result in more connection. But as with many of the practices in this book, we must accept feeling somewhat (or even deeply) uncomfortable in order to achieve full aliveness and authenticity.

Discomfort is part of life, and is something to be celebrated along with all the other human emotions and sensations. Telling the truth can feel good and relieving once we speak it, but beforehand, it often feels scary. Through the practice of Reveal Your Experience, we proactively welcome and embrace this discomfort, trusting that there can be no *real* connection without truth.

To skillfully reveal ourselves takes practice. It's best to start out by revealing small things, so that people around us can adjust to this new mode of connection. One pitfall of Authentic Relating can be that we suddenly start dropping "truth bombs," expecting others to instantly adapt to our newfound authenticity. It's important to remember that not all the people in your life will have the same understanding and skills, and integrating them can take some adjustment on both sides.

AR POWER TOOL
May I Reveal Something to You?

The heart of Authentic Relating is our courage to express: to have the hard conversation and reveal the *thing* we might not normally share. And the "belly" of Authentic Relating is our ability to receive: to absorb the nourishment of safety and belonging that comes with being known and seen. The question, *May I reveal something to you?* is often the perfect tool for both!

For some of us, requesting listening and attention can already be a vulnerable request. Of course, waiting around for other people to get curious about you is also *not* a great strategy to be known and met! This Olin Miller quote really drives this point home: "You probably wouldn't worry about what people think of you if you could know how seldom they do!"

In making this request, we get consent from the other in a collaborative way. Not only does it show them respect, it gives all parties the choice to invest or not in the exchange. It also is a gentle step into expressing our vulnerability, which, for many of us, is scary territory.

Asking the question and paying close attention to the response can create a doorway for a new type of conversation in the relationship. Use this tool often, and you may find people turning toward you with more softness and care.

Practice 4: Own Your Experience

Now that we've discussed how to reveal our experience, let's explore the dynamic practice of taking ownership of it. *Own Your Experience* means we take responsibility (both internally and externally) for our thoughts, emotions, and beliefs about the world—and their effects on ourselves and the people around us.

Owning our experience is an art form, and one of the more difficult practices of Authentic Relating. When we endeavor to own our experience fully, we come face-to-face with ourselves, and looking into this mirror can be uncomfortable. This is because the way we express ourselves is a mirror of our emotional maturity. We must be prepared to love ourselves enough to take full responsibility for our own emotional growth. This is no small feat—but the effort is very much worth it.

The most disempowered times of our lives are when we play the role of the victim, blaming people and situations around us for our feelings and circumstances. On the other hand, the most empowered times are those when we take responsibility for our experience, and for our contribution to our circumstances.

For example, rather than saying, "You made me mad!" we might say, "I'm feeling angry. Are you open to me sharing how I was affected by your behavior?" The difference between these two expressions is obvious. The former blames another for your experience; the latter acknowledges whatever has occurred as a "co-creation" between two people.

In practicing owning our experience, we will inevitably encounter the part of us that doesn't want to take responsibility—the part that wants to blame, simply because it feels easier to do so. Each of us has this internal victim, developed from unmet childhood needs. Getting in touch with this victim's voice can be an important step in taking more ownership in our lives.

As an aside, many parents report that their children take to Authentic Relating quickly and easily, except for one particular practice: owning their experience! Taking responsibility for emotional states isn't something children can easily do. Their growing nervous systems are quickly overwhelmed by their emotions, so they find ways to discharge and regulate that intensity. Often, this may look like blaming siblings or an external circumstance, to avoid the immediate challenge of facing a self-growth moment.

As adults, when we feel pressured or threatened, we may revert to more childish behaviors, including blaming others. Forgoing responsibility is a phase we all go through when we are young, but as developed adults creating healthy communities, we can—and should—develop a sense of accountability. Try these steps the next time you find yourself wanting to blame someone else for an experience you're having.

Step 1: Notice How You're Avoiding Ownership

Become aware of words or behaviors that indicate a lack of ownership or personal responsibility. Ask yourself, "How might I be judging or blaming others? Am I wanting someone or something to change to make me feel something different?"

Step 2: Ask Yourself: *What are my wants and needs?*

Once we are able to see that we not only want, but perhaps *expect*, others to act in certain ways, we realize that getting our needs met ultimately stems from our own communication and actions. This is because only *we* can determine what our needs actually *are*. Instead of expecting others to change, we can ask, "How can I create a better situation, by bringing more of my own values to the table?"

Step 3: Communicate and Act

As Gandhi said, "Be the change you wish to see in the world". With a deeper sense of our needs and our values, we can begin to act and communicate from that place. In Step 3, we further take responsibility to translate our insights into action.

Important note on Step 3: Marshall Rosenberg's "Nonviolent Communication" (or NVC) is a model of communication and approach to living that has influenced the cultural zeitgeist toward deeper empathy and understanding over the last five decades.[8] This has laid the foundation for using "I statements": a simple practice of owning one's experience. This is a general tip around starting sentences with "I" instead of "you": "I see," "I feel," "I want," or "I need," for example. It is true that this is a great start in taking ownership, though unfortunately this practice can be twisted to surreptitiously cast blame or shirk responsibility. For example, we can still say, "I feel like you're being selfish!" or, "I need you to stop manipulating me!" As you can see, using "I statements" has the potential to mask blame or an unowned experience.

---

8   Rosenberg, Marshall B. *Nonviolent Communication: a Language of Life: Create Your Life, Your Relationships and Your World in Harmony with Your Values.* 2003.

AR POWER TOOL
Acknowledge Your Impact, *or* Admit Your Sh!t

Whenever we discuss our weaknesses honestly (at least, as best as we can understand them), we invite authenticity. Further, we potentially transform something that could be disconnecting into deeper connection with others. Admitting our sh!t is an opening to feedback, as well as an invitation for reciprocal vulnerability—and though it may sound counterintuitive, this vulnerability is where we truly grow. In facing this discomfort, we open the doorway to more fulfilling relationships.

Especially when there is a power differential, acknowledging the potential impact that you have on others can have a magical effect on the relationship. With this tool, we can create a culture of authenticity, even in the face of the parts of our personalities that have caused us grief. Examples:

Sometimes I'm not great at details when I'm on the go. Could you help me remember to check that we have everything before the meeting on Saturday?

Often I get into a serious mode where I feel stiff. I notice you laugh a lot. How do you keep a relaxed attitude?

I think of myself as a good friend, but I sometimes really struggle with returning messages. Can you let me know if that impacts you in a negative way?

Practice 5: Honor Self and Other

Honor Self and Other is an agreement of mutual respect that is necessary for any healthy connection to take root and thrive. Of course, maintaining respect and consideration for everyone is more complicated than it sounds, especially in times of conflict. Even though the ultimate goal is to be able to consistently honor both ourselves and others at the same time, many of us start out practicing these skills independently.

For example, many of us have a pattern of overriding or masking our true responses and thoughts in order to feel accepted by others. We sweep things under the rug, unwilling (or unable) to reveal ourselves. In this place, we are not truly honoring ourselves—and unfortunately, any sense of love and acceptance we might be gaining from this relational dynamic comes at the cost of our dignity, energy, and authenticity. When we find ourselves caught in this pattern, we can begin by simply asking, "Am I aware of my feelings and desires right now? Am I going along with others out of habit?"

On the other hand, some of us have developed the opposite pattern: We enter into a highly postured state in conflict situations and forget to honor others. We might be very connected with our own desires and needs in these moments, but in this more selfish place, we're more likely to make assumptions about others and disregard their experiences. When we find ourselves in this place, we can ask ourselves, "Am I failing to notice the others in this situation? To what degree am I in touch with *their* needs and feelings right now?"

Even if we are able to hold others' perspectives as being just as valuable as our own, sometimes the wants and needs of others will be oppositional to our own. Indeed, *Honor Self and Other* doesn't mean both sides will always get "their way." Rather, it is the willingness to have a constructive conversation, where both are seen, heard and validated.

When we embody this practice of honoring ourselves and others, we invite dignity and humility in the face of conflict—which brings us to the formula that forms the heart of this book.

If Conflict = Emotional Energy,
and Dignity + Humility = Transformation,
then Dignity + Humility During Conflict =
Transformation of Emotional Energy

Once we begin to view conflict as a doorway to greater connection, clarity, teamwork, and energy, a simple yet monumental shift occurs. The internal messages of, "This should not be happening!" or "Who is to blame here?" begin to shift to, "What is happening here?" and "What growth, connection, or clarity can come from handling this with skill?"

AR POWER TOOL
The Check-in

This might be the simplest of all AR tools, yet it is surprisingly powerful in its effect. Simply allocate some time at the beginning of a hangout, party, group interaction, meeting, or even a one-to-one coffee date with a friend, and use that time for a check-in.

In this process, each person is given a set amount of time to speak freely about what is present for them: what's going on in their life and what they are aware of in the present moment.

Even doing this for a brief amount of time can dramatically change the tone of any interaction. Not only do we bring ourselves into the now and allow ourselves to be seen, we discover that all of us are filled with unprocessed experiences, which are obviously or subtly shaping our current realities.

By spending time checking in with each person, we give our system time to shift out of whatever was happening before into what is happening now. By doing so, we release small amounts of energy, which allows us to be more productive and present with each other.

In professional settings, we can even create a culture of checking in: allocating one or two minutes for each person to speak before meetings. Over time, this can help to create an atmosphere of greater authenticity in our workplaces.

Chapter 4
CONNECTING TO SELF

———————

Know Thyself.

—SOCRATES

I do not show this skin for you,
I show myself to know myself.

—AYLA NEREO

Who we are at the very core of our being is the subject of the entire fields of philosophy and spirituality. In service of keeping our exploration practical and applicable to our relationships, we will merely dip our toe in these deep waters. Authentic Relating has a very simple answer to the age-old question of what it means to be human: We are first and foremost the inner relationship we have with ourselves. We have many inner voices, tugging and pulling us this way and that. Who and what we are, then, is the integrated voice of all our myriad of parts. That is, we *are* our Connection to Self.

A great deal of modern thinking, especially in the West, has been influenced by the assembly line and the rise of the machine. Modernization has led to much progress in terms of efficiency and productivity, but this hasn't come without its costs. We have been conditioned, by our culture, to seek constant improvement, success, and individualism—and this seeking affects us more than we may recognize.

You and I are not machines. Human beings are not machines. Our achievements rarely follow linear paths. A machine, theoretically, could live forever and learn to do everything perfectly, but that is not the human fate. We are natural and we are alive, having far more in common with the plants and animals around us than the devices and machines we now rely on so heavily.

There are many ways in which we are limited, whether we care to admit this or not. This idea of limits tends to be unpopular in our culture of personal growth, which glorifies achievement and the idea that we can do anything we put our minds to. In the West, we seem to be in an all-out war against the idea of human limitation. This individualistic culture of success, aided by social media and the "selfie," encourages us to put our "best" selves forward as much as possible.

For many of us, this leads to a deep-seated desire (or even expectation) to be some kind of superhero. Inevitably, we feel shame when we fail to meet these standards. We hide our faults and inadequacies, and end up in posture, grandiosity, and self-hatred. What a mess!

Much of the beauty of Authentic Relating is in recognizing that who we are, as we are, is okay. Nothing needs to be changed, fixed, or improved. In fact, this is a root understanding of many spiritual and religious practices. Connection to ourselves *exactly* as we are is the most fertile source for personal growth. In this moment, can you truly believe you are okay exactly as you are? For many of us, this can be a radical act, so I invite you to simply try it on and consider it. Attempting to fix or improve ourselves without a strong foundation of self-acceptance tends to hinder our growth, not help it.

Organic Growth

You are a unique arising in the entirety of human history. Just like the clichéd snowflake, every human being is distinct. Because of this uniqueness, no one can tell you a damn thing about how to relate to yourself! (There are, of course, useful guides, one of which this book attempts to be.) In order to deeply connect with ourselves, we must look within and sort through all the energies, emotions, and voices we find in there. This is what is known as "inner work."

Why would we do this work? Understanding our organic nature as individuals is essential to unlocking our gifts. Yet to our detriment, we tend to measure ourselves against outer gauges of success, instead of tuning into our true nature. Comparison with others can be very useful in our younger years, to learn about the world and what is possible, but ultimately it doesn't work in motivating us toward sustainable, deep growth. Relying on this type of comparison will always leave us underdeveloped, and prevent our gifts from growing fully.

We can't manipulate ourselves into being like our heroes and celebrities. Our true selves are utterly unique, and must be discovered through inner work. If we view ourselves as machines or projects to be subjected to constant improvement, we will constantly be assessing whether something in us is right or wrong, or good enough. Comparison invokes a certain type of "either/or" thinking, while true growth of the self occurs in an atmosphere of creativity and nurturing. At the same time, the mind's base function is to judge the past (that is, to learn) so that it may project future possibilities, and help ensure our physical survival. So, we certainly don't want to throw the baby out with the bathwater.

Critical judgment is a highly useful and necessary human capacity. Another word for this is "discernment." This capacity is what has allowed us to do everything from building infrastructures and vehicles, to peering into the very molecules that make up our bodies and our world. Understanding organic growth simply means understanding that our critical mind can be counterproductive when it comes to matters of the heart. Our emotions and relationships do not live by the same rules as, say, physics or math.

Without the emotional intelligence to balance our critical mind, our relationships will certainly suffer greatly. The critical mind benefits relationships when we use it to identify areas for learning and growth. But once we've identified these, we must then enter the territory of our heart and body—which speak an entirely different language. As discussed in Chapter 2, embodiment is the universal translator, which is why Authentic Relating is an embodied practice. It connects the many facets of our intelligence, creating pathways of communication between them.

Exploring the Critical Mind

Take a moment to experience this. For 30 seconds—*but no more*—allow yourself to criticize and judge a behavior or personality trait you have. What does this feel like in your body? How does this affect your emotions? If you're like me, self-judgment feels like sh!t. It's demoralizing. When I entertain such thoughts, I tend to shrink and collapse.

When we notice ourselves thinking cynically or judgmentally in this way, we can bring ourselves back to a clearer line of thinking by simply taking a deep breath and feeling the expansion of our lungs. This immediate reminder of the organic, living nature of our beings is immediately available to us from our first breath to our last. Even when we are shaky with emotion or other distractions, we can always call ourselves back into connection with self by simply feeling our breath.

If we can connect with the natural seed of our being in this way, watering and shining light on it with care, it will flower and bear the fruit of our natural gifts. This kind of self-connection takes time and loving attention, but the reward in our relationships with others is well worth the investment. We can only be as supportive and authentic in our relationships with others as we can be in our relationship with ourselves.

AR POWER TOOL
Mirror Work

This deceptively simple practice can do some serious heavy lifting in connecting to self—it might even change your life. Does this sound too good to be true? Try it and find out.

Find a quiet place with a mirror where you can speak freely, and set a timer for five minutes (or whatever length of time you choose). Look yourself in the eyes, and have an honest "conversation." You might begin by simply saying hello to yourself, and naming your immediate thoughts and emotions. As you connect to yourself in this most literal of ways, simply notice what happens.

Many people find that the emotions they experience while in direct contact with themselves are complex and enlightening. As best you can, relax into the process and be open to the healing power of devoting time to your relationship with yourself.

Relationship as a Pathway for Growth

The relationship we have with ourselves is not just a core piece of who we are; it *is* who we are. The emotional tone and energy of that connection affects us and everyone around us, and is the single constant we bring into every other sphere of our lives. If we want to expand our possibilities and overcome our limitations in connection with others, our connection with self is the first place to start.

To the extent that we fail to pay attention to and deepen this primary relationship with ourselves, our other connections will be surface-level and prone to reactivity. Like any other relationship, our connection with self requires time and energy to nurture. But ultimately, this is the first step on the pathway to experiencing relationship as growth.

A healthy relationship with yourself goes far beyond the self-care advocated in many self-help circles. It's true that cultivating a rich relationship with yourself might sometimes look like bubble baths and walking around the block for a breath of fresh air. But a truly deep connection to self requires a measure of self-care that, for many of us, is unfamiliar or even uncomfortable. Often we avoid looking inside because of the emotional pain we know we'll find when we delve into our depths. And yet, liberating this pain also liberates our ability to feel the full range of human emotions—including joy. Over time, we can massage away our emotional scar tissue, by approaching our hurts, wounds, and self-judgments with a gentle touch.

AR POWER TOOL
"Connect to Self" Meditation

Connecting to Self is a focusing practice that helps us become more aware of ourselves, so that we may bring that deeper sense of self into our connection with others. Influenced by a variety of meditation practices, this Authentic Relating version is characterized by a lack of orientation to a particular goal. Rather than trying to reach a certain state (inner peace, for example), the practice of Connecting to Self is merely about noticing what is present. Whether our inner state is calm, excited, anxious, or sad is irrelevant. We simply notice, and welcome whatever arises as a meaningful part of our experience.

Cues for Individual or Facilitated Practice

- Feel your feet on the ground.
- Connect with your breath.
- Notice what is happening for you at this moment emotionally, physically and mentally.
- Remember: Nothing needs to be fixed or changed. Any desire to fix or change is simply something else to notice.
- Give it all some space, and take a few deep breaths.
- You can stretch your toes or move a little bit… whatever you feel you might need to attune more deeply with yourself.

Some meditation techniques are based on structure, encouraging physical stillness and good posture. Such practices aim to build a capacity for attention or focus. The *Connect to Self*

Authentic Relating meditation intends instead to guide us through connecting with all that we are in the moment. That is why stretching and making small slow movements are welcomed in this meditation. Even yawning or sighing is allowed if those things help you become more attuned to your present moment experience.

The purpose of this practice is to help us digest and metabolize our experience, so that we can be more present and whole in our lives and relationships. It is often said that in this place of deeper connection with ourselves, there is more space for connection with others.

Growth from Wholeness

It makes sense that many of us shy away from inner work. After all, if we really look inside, we might find a lot of self-criticism and emotional pain. In attempting to find connection with ourselves, we're bound to first discover a lot of disconnection. Try ignoring your best friend or spouse for more than a day—the relationship goes downhill pretty fast! Yet many of us haven't cultivated a strong relationship with self, and have neglected our own emotional needs for months or even years.

The solution to disconnection from self is twofold. First, we must understand that we are *organic beings* (not machines!), and second, we must practice acceptance of whatever we are experiencing. In other words, we can only grow from where we're planted.

So much of personal growth culture gets this understanding backward, purporting to give us tools to improve ourselves (often in the guise of "development"). We don't need a class, book, exercise routine, or workshop to help us "fix ourselves." Organic growth and self-improvement strategies are two different things. From the vantage point of organic growth, we connect with ourselves as we are, trusting that we are already whole. Instead of seeking to change ourselves, we choose to foster intimacy with ourselves *as we are*, giving ourselves time and space to observe and inquire into our authentic experience in each moment. This practice cultivates self-love, dignity, and peace.

Self-intimacy is something no one can teach us, no matter how wise they may be. We must take that inward journey by ourselves and for ourselves. One of the rewards for practicing authenticity is that we get to be and know ourselves more fully through each interaction we have with others. Authentic Relating is not a method to manipulate ourselves or our experience of the external world. It is a practice and a way of living, for becoming more honest, transparent, and connected. As it turns out, this process is far more satisfying than molding ourselves into something we think the world will accept, or attempting to mold others to be more acceptable to us.

AR POWER TOOL
Emotional Clarity

This tool is especially essential for navigating conflict. Us humans often have many conflicting emotions and thoughts—sometimes one right after the other. If you find yourself totally confused about a relationship, you are not alone! Simply *knowing* that you are unclear can actually help move you towards a more resourced place.

Connection to self, in tangible terms, means that we have the ability to identify our wants, needs, and feelings, and to know what to do with them. Very often, when in the midst of a confusing experience, the best next step is to create some space and time to sort through your emotions. When there is an acute challenge in a relationship, follow these steps to cultivate emotional regulation.

Step 1: Identify where you feel a lack of emotional clarity. Is this a big thing? Intense anger or a minor annoyance? Sadness or fear? Who are the people involved and what are the different variables? Practice this simple self-assessment to identify all the elements that need to be sorted.

Step 2: Communicate to the person you're feeling challenged with that you need some space so you can find more clarity. This may take some courage! That's why embracing discomfort is an important element of Authentic Relating. Each instance of authentically expressing with another helps us build that capacity.

Step 3: Depending on the intensity of the feelings you're experiencing, take an hour, day, or week away from the relationship. Use this time to identify what you need and what might be getting in the way. (Some examples of needs: to be listened to or validated, to have boundaries respected, to receive honesty from others, to be acknowledged for work we have done.)

Step 4: Once we're clear, we can communicate—letting go of the need to do so "perfectly." Remember, it's only human to oscillate between clarity and confusion.

Note: There will of course be times when others cannot or do not wish to meet our requests. This may lead us to feel disappointed, angry, ashamed, or just plain devastated. How to manage these kinds of experiences is something we'll delve into further in Part III of this book.

While navigating this landscape of emotional needs can be tricky, learning to do so skillfully brings us greater intimacy with others and ourselves. When we choose to stop hiding our feelings from those close to us, and practice asking for what we need, more of our authentic selves become available to our relationships—and the opportunity is created for others to reciprocate.

PART II

GAMES TO GROW
EMOTIONAL INTELLIGENCE:
The Pedagogy
of Authentic Relating

Simply put, *pedagogy* is the study of the best way to teach something, so that others can truly absorb it and put it into practice. Every good teacher spends a portion of their post-graduate time studying how their particular subject is best learned by others. Every knowledge base has specific learning methods to convey information most easily—and as we've been exploring, relational abilities are learned skills.

In Part III, we will explore the transformation of conflict into abundant, free energy, using these relational skills. But first, let's delve into the pedagogy of AR, or the "how" of increasing our emotional intelligence.

Why Do We Practice These Skills by Playing Games?

Authentic Relating aims to cultivate presence, appreciation, and curiosity—all in service of deepening our self and relational knowledge. Our social wellbeing is a natural outflow of our social awareness. While the goal of learning authentic relationships is at the heart of this practice, building and creating community is a natural byproduct. We learn by being together, and fun and connection are intrinsic to the AR way.

Authentic Relating "Games Nights" are held weekly in dozens of cities all over the world, drawing participants from a wide range of ages, backgrounds, and systems of belief. Since 2005, this largely decentralized movement has grown in leaps and bounds, expanding to meet our culture's ever-deepening need for more "alive" and authentic connections.

The games vary across the globe, with some key design consistencies. However played, they are designed to create novel experiences that interrupt our habitual ways of being, and opportunities to stretch ourselves emotionally, mentally, and relationally. Some of these games might seem similar to exercises found in other personal development workshops—though we expressly call them "games" to encourage playful curiosity. Even AR Games that are more serious in nature can be approached with an attitude of experimentation that empowers learning.

Aside from being fun, these games can incite profound social-emotional learning (the development of capacities such as empathy, self-awareness, and emotional regulation). When we become more aware of our impact on others (and others' impacts on us), we become more empowered and at choice in how we show up in connection. This can become a "feedback loop" that provides further fuel for this growth. Chapter 8 explores more of the power of these feedback loops through the teachings on *hologram*.

We will explore three core games in this section of the book: one each for *presence, appreciation,* and *curiosity.* Note that any game instructions are presented in such a way as to be used by a "facilitator"—though a formally facilitated environment is not necessary. Try playing these games with friends or family, or in more professional or structured contexts. For additional games (as well as other resources), see the appendix at the end of the book.

Chapter 5
PRESENCE

In presence, we can know ourselves in a way that is authentic,
which means that we are knowing what is real in us. When we
feel presence, we are experiencing our underlying reality.

—A.H. ALMAAS

What happens when you think of the word "home"? For
many of us, it brings to mind a feeling of being rested, right
here and right now. When we are embodied, we feel at home
within ourselves, and can carry that energy into our experiences with others wherever we go. We feel resourceful and
have plenty to share and contribute to others. We relate with
others from a place of feeling that we are enough, without
impulsively seeking reassurance from the outside world. In
such states, you could say that we *are* reassurance itself. This
is what we call *presence*: an energetic frequency of solidness
that emanates from our core, and can feel boundless.

Presence is a well-studied topic. From Csikszentmihalyi's
studies on flow,[9] to the role of mindfulness in medicine and

---

9   Csikszentmihalyi, Mihaly. *Flow: the Psychology of Optimal Experience.* Harper Row,
    2009.

healthcare through the work of Jon Kabat-Zinn,[10] the idea of presence seems to show up everywhere. It's often discussed in conjunction with *awareness* or *mindfulness*. These concepts mean different things to different people, so let's begin with an experience that can inform our discussion.

A Simple Practice to Experience Presence

- Take several moments to feel your breath enter and leave your nose as you breathe. Slow down, pause, and feel the simplicity of the sensations of breath at the nostrils.
- Now take a few moments to feel your chest rise and fall, as you breathe in and out.
- After another 10 seconds or so, try placing your attention on your feet and toes for a couple of breaths. Next, notice your hands and the sensations there. Feel the temperature of the air on your skin.
- Next, see if you can be aware of your whole body, and after a couple of breaths here, expand your awareness to include sights and sounds. Become aware of the sensations on your skin and the sounds around you—perhaps distant noise from the street outside, or others in the next room. Notice the quality of light in the room, and the colors and shapes of the objects. Keep your attention open and diffuse.

The value of such a simple exercise is often overlooked. Once we learn to directly practice presence, this skill can be deeply

---

10· Kabat-Zinn, Jon. "Mindfulness-Based Interventions in Context: Past, Present, and Future." *Clinical Psychology: Science and Practice*, vol. 10, no. 2, 2003, pp. 144–156., doi:10.1093/clipsy.bpg016.

integrated, allowing us to feel greater ease and flow with our surroundings, no matter the circumstance. In fact, Ellen Langer, sometimes referred to as the "mother of mindfulness," has found that this state (which she defines simply as "actively noticing things") can lead to increased health, competence, and happiness.[11] In this way, presence can become an ordinary superpower!

Noticing Nuance to Build Emotional Muscles

Many Authentic Relating Games are perspective-shifting exercises that increase our capacity to be aware of our own feelings, or our "felt sense" of reality. We can think of both our feelings themselves and our awareness of them as the emotional muscles we are developing, and the foundations of healthy and skillful communication. Think of the heart muscle; it's always beating. Though we only occasionally become aware of that beating on our own, we can choose to put our attention here intentionally.

Attuning to this present moment with our "felt sense" is a practice that takes time to master. At first, navigating your emotional landscape may seem overwhelming: a lake that you've just dived into. You may not know which way is up or down, and if the lake is murky, it can take some time to get your bearings. This is where we can pair our "felt sense" with our "witnessing awareness." Imagine that same lake, but rather than diving head-first into its waters, you instead sit on its banks, simply observing. This latter practice can lend more objectivity to our emotional lives.

---

11 Langer, Ellen. Interview with Krista Tippett. *On Being*, 29 May. 2014.

These two basic muscles of feeling and witnessing are like a bicep and tricep. They work together in opposing ways, exercising both our "objective" and "subjective" senses of reality. The felt sense allows us to notice the details and nuance of an experience, while the witnessing awareness prevents us from getting lost in it. This can become a type of cycle, in which the capacity to be with our reality more "objectively" then enables us to experience it with deeper acuity and sensitivity.

Over time, this can become a type of intuition training. And despite Western culture's valuation of rational intelligence and logic above all, I believe many of us know in our hearts that intuition is at least equally important. This is because intuition is a combination of our thinking *and* feeling capacities: When we connect more deeply with our bodies and hearts, we free up more space to be mentally present. This is the access point to our intuitive voice.

AR POWER TOOL
Naming Emotions

All of us get stuck in our heads—and from time to time, can be totally disconnected from our emotional experience. As human beings, it's normal for us to compartmentalize all the feelings that we don't have the energy to deal with right away.

Once we have the time and space to look at the things we've been repressing, one of the most powerful ways to process our emotions is simply to name them. Here's how to do it:

1. Set aside two to five minutes (or more, depending on the intensity of your feelings).

2. Get comfortable, either sitting or lying down.

3. Recall an intense experience that happened recently, or a current situation in your life that has some emotional activation.

4. Put your hand on your chest and name (internally or out loud) whatever emotions have come up for you in this situation. For example, "Right now, I am feeling sad."

5. As best you can, simply feel the feeling. Then take a breath, and elaborate if wanted (e.g., "I'm feeling sad because of a recent loss," or, "I'm feeling anxious because of a situation at work").

The statements that we make are intentionally simple. They are a verbal anchor pointing towards the feeling. We want to avoid any tendency to let our thoughts "play out" the story, and this anchor connects our mental worlds with the worlds of our senses and hearts. Through acknowledging how we really feel without giving way to stories, we give our emotions space.

You can follow this pattern for any uncomfortable experience, whenever you have time and want to attend to your emotions. Our presence is what allows for integration—and in this way, we can arrive at a more resourced and regulated place.

Illuminating the Shadow to Increase Presence

As we noted earlier, aspects of ourselves that we would normally hide, repress, or deny (to ourselves and/or to others) can be collectively referred to as *the shadow self*. Our shadow selves include all of these qualities, as well as the ways in which we hide them. In our belief that these qualities are undesirable, we can end up spending much of our lives playing games of "hide and seek," trying to obscure them from others.

The problem is that such denial requires a tremendous amount of emotional energy. We become less present, creating a downward spiral that greatly diminishes our potential for full connection. To the extent that we use our emotional-mental bandwidth to obscure these parts from others, we have less energy and attention available for each moment; thus, misunderstandings and relational drama are more likely to ensue.

The solution starts with noticing what is happening right now, in all its fullness—even if that is something as seemingly inconsequential as an itchy toe or a mild feeling of awkwardness.

This simplicity is by no means easy. How do we become aware of what we are not aware of? The funny thing about presence is that the best way to develop it is to repeatedly notice when we are *not* present! By shining the light of our presence into the shadow of suppressed and repressed emotions, thoughts, and tendencies, we automatically free up energy that we can then use to generate deeper connections.

Through addressing our shadows, we build our capacity to include "the full human"—at work, at home, and in all our important relationships. In this way, we can create an ever-widening culture of authenticity, where we can share what is truly happening for us underneath the surface.

AR POWER TOOL
The Charge Scale

The Charge Scale is a quick check for any internal emotional state we are experiencing. When used within a group, this tool can quickly open up a new depth of connection, while increasing a sense of overall group cohesion.

In a group of any size, each person takes a turn sharing a number from one to 10. This number represents how "activated" or charged the person is feeling on that day. Higher numbers indicate more intense and challenging emotional states like grief or anger, whereas lower numbers indicate feeling more calm, pleasant or resourced. What's important is that the number reflects the present moment, even if we wish things felt different. A sentence or two can also be included for additional context. For example:

This morning, I'm a one. Feeling happy, peaceful, and ready.

I'm about a four today. I feel productive and clear, but also stressed about some communication breakdowns I'm having with colleagues.

I'm a seven, and a little bit of a wreck. My partner and I had a fight before I left the house this morning, and it's been hard to get my head in the game today.

The Charge Scale exercises several "emotional muscles," including self-assessment and transparency. Over time, through simply taking our emotional temperatures and sharing them with each other, we normalize more of the full range of our experience, which can eventually transform the culture as a whole.

Note: This tool is a type of "check-in" which we covered at the end of Chapter 3. Assessing our internal state and letting others know what is happening for us is central to the practice of AR, and there are many variations and styles of check-in.

The Three Levels of Communication

The *Three Levels of Communication* have been around since the beginning of Authentic Relating. They are important not only in navigating toward the type of connection that is the most appropriate or nourishing in the moment, but also as a tool for staying intentional in our interactions with others. These three levels are *informational, personal,* and *relational.* As you'll see, the level of present-moment awareness increases with each level.

Informational

Informational communication is centered around facts. When we're conversing on this level, we're concerned with concrete "reality": the weather, sports, hobbies, what we ate for breakfast, and all things related to the logistics of our lives. Informational communication lives in the past and the future, and tends to make up the vast majority of our conversations. While this type of relating is useful and necessary in many social settings, it can also feel dull, lifeless, and perfunctory. For this reason, it's also sometimes colloquially labeled as "small talk."

If questions like, "What do you do?", "Where did you go to school?", and "Do you have kids?" are your main repertoire for getting to know someone, the three levels can help you navigate conversations into deeper territory.

Personal

This level moves one step closer to the core of who we are. One way to think of this layer is how we *feel* about everything in the informational layer: our emotions, values, motivations, memories, dreams, and hopes for the future. The *personal* is the fabric and the story of our lives. It's, "How do you *feel* about your job?" or "What's it *like* for you to have kids?"

Almost all people crave more of the personal, because it is on this level that we can begin to feel a nourishing sense of belonging. Unfortunately, the socialized default tends to be informational, which can sometimes lead us to perceive others (or ourselves) as boring or shallow. The much more exciting reality is that people become more *interesting* when we ourselves become more *interested*. With this understanding, we can *choose* to be more curious about others, and watch how our interactions become richer as a result.

Relational

The final level of communication is known as *relational*. This level happens when both parties are exchanging observations and feelings about what's happening in connection *right now*. Where the personal and informational levels focus on the past and future, the relational level is all about the present moment. I share what it's like for me to be with you, and you share what it's like for you to be with me. It's, "What's it like to share with me that you hate your job?" or "Hearing you say that, I'm noticing my own deep desire to be a parent."

Relational communication is a type of intimacy that is both nourishing and vital, in a world starving for connection. When we reveal *how* we are experiencing the connection itself, a deep, core need of being seen and heard is met. When another reciprocates, compassion and empathy flow. This is the power of the third level of communication.

The Noticing Game

The Noticing Game is a foundational and highly adaptable AR exercise. It allows us to uncover what is deeply present, but usually unspoken. These aren't "secrets," necessarily, but may be things that are thought of as too small or obvious to mention in an interaction. Despite their simplicity, exposing such observations can bring about extraordinary freedom for participants. "You mean I can say *that*?!" Yes, you can say anything. "You mean, you have an itchy toe when I'm thinking about the poison ivy reaction I had last month?" In this game, there are no limits to the strange little details we can discover in connection.

Typically, the Noticing Game is practiced in pairs. Once people have partnered up, a facilitator will prompt Person A of the pair to say, "Being with you, I notice…" Person A will then complete the sentence with something they are noticing. This can be guided by the facilitator asking the participants to focus their observations in some way—on physical sensations, emotions, or thoughts—or can be more free-form, spanning any of these categories.

Person B will then respond with, "Being with you, I notice…" and will then complete the sentence with whatever is present (which may or may not be directly related to what was just shared). Formatting the responses in this way allows players to respond to each other's shared communication (or "shares") in a dynamic exchange, weaving back and forth.

The point of this game is to give players an opportunity to enter an open-ended, and present-moment, relational space. Here, anything goes—from the concrete to the spiritual, the mundane to the bizarre. Exploring in this way is a doorway to presence. And this is where all of the energy, juice, and aliveness is. By saying the thing that's right under our nose, sometimes we can "unstick" ourselves from the rigidity of old relational patterns, and get into an experience of flow with another person—no matter who they are.

Tips for Facilitating the Noticing Game

Categories

The open-ended nature of this game can be confusing for people new to AR, so it can be helpful to ask participants to notice things in particular categories. For example, you (as the facilitator) might suggest physical sensations, objective observations about the other person or oneself, emotions, or recurring thoughts. Any selected topic or theme can become the object of the game.

Beginning the Game

Begin by leading with a period of silent eye contact between partners (choosing an appropriate duration for your audience and their experience level). This builds anticipation for what is to come and deepens present-moment connection. As the facilitator, you can even slow down your rate of speaking a bit during this time, to help players drop into a space of deeper attention and noticing.

Stay Present

While leading the Noticing Game, stay present to how simple and profound it can be. Holding this in your facilitation-awareness can help participants appreciate the magic of simply noticing what is arising now.

Variations

"Hearing that, I notice..."

The game (like the original) is played "ping-pong" style, with the exchange going back and forth between two people. The response is usually, but not always related to the original share (e.g. "Being with you, I notice I feel shy." "Hearing that, I notice I become a little careful and wonder how I can connect with you.").

All-In

Going around in a circle, each person shares what they notice in the moment. This can be a way to bring everyone's voice into the group, or serve as a warm-up for a small group practice like The Now Game (see the appendix for additional games).

Noticing Check-In

In pairs, each person has two minutes to share what they are noticing "at the top of their awareness," in a range of categories (e.g. sensations, objective observations, curiosities). Their partner simply witnesses the open-ended inquiry. The person who goes first starts with the phrase, "Right now, I notice…" and continues to complete this sentence until the time is up. Then, switch roles.

Chapter 6

APPRECIATION

Everything is a gift. The degree to which we are awake to this truth is a measure of our gratefulness, and gratefulness is a measure of our aliveness.

—DAVID STEINDL-RAST

On January 13th, 2020, a 46-second video of a lone man on a London park bench singing Bon Jovi went viral. It wasn't because he was a great singer—it was because this one exuberant voice sparked an entire park to join together in song. Quickly, the video acquired nearly 2 million views, and a slew of comments from strangers including, "This might be the closest humanity has gotten towards world peace."[12]

Your heart is powerful. So is mine. The energy generated from one delightful spirit can shift an entire crowd to joy. The energy we generate together when our hearts are in resonance can start movements, and even change the world. How, then, do we access the power of our hearts? Like the

---

12 "Jon Bon Jovi Park Singing by a Guy." *YouTube*, uploaded by Matej Priteržnik, 13 Jan 2020, www.youtube.com/watch?v=LtoQY7i3kH0.

Bon Jovi fan in the London park, it begins with finding our joy and following it.

Our heart energy is contagious and potent for creating goodness in the world. So how do we grow this heart energy? Observing those who have a high degree of "heart intelligence," it becomes apparent that a fulfilling life begins with appreciation. The word "appreciation" can describe, A) the pleasure of recognition, B) full understanding, C) gratitude, and D) the increase in perceived value over time. Each of these definitions, I believe, come together to form a full picture of what appreciation means in the world of Authentic Relating. Let's illuminate these meanings one at a time.

The pleasure of recognition: The simple pleasure of recognizing and enjoying the qualities of a person, place, or thing is perhaps one of the easiest emotions for us to observe in ourselves—and when we experience this with others, its effects can be cumulative. Think of the appreciation of a crowd at a concert feeding on itself—and ultimately being reflected back in the performance of the artist in front of them. The more people feel and express their appreciation simultaneously, the more the rest of the group can reach this state naturally. As you might recall from the Harvard study mentioned earlier, our happiness in life is directly linked to the quality of our relationships—and sharing these pleasures with others is an excellent tool for improving that quality.

Full understanding: Appreciation also means to fully understand a situation or problem, and what it involves. In the book *Stranger in a Strange Land,* Robert Heinlein coins the term "grok," which means to understand something so thoroughly that we know it intuitively.[13] Essentially, to "grok" is to know something so deeply that we become a part of it and merge with it.

If we "grok" our lives, the people in it, and the beauty of the natural world around us, our natural response is overwhelming gratitude. Our lives become a rich tapestry of deeply fulfilling experiences, because we appreciate everything, no matter the content or circumstance. Exercising the heart in this way is key to building emotional intelligence over time, and accessing its true power.

Gratitude: Another important part of appreciation is actively practicing gratitude. In the field of Positive Psychology, championed by Martin Seligman and others,[14] gratitude has been shown to be strongly and consistently associated with greater overall wellbeing.[15] I believe if we take a closer look, we'll see that gratitude has an actual, physical effect on our heart and viscera. And it's not only the "good" things in our lives that we can practice gratitude for—it's *everything.*

Increase in perceived value over time: Finally, appreciation can mean the increase of value over time. Our hearts have the power to invest in connections and groups in such deep ways that we can feel the positive effects for years, even if we can't see them with our eyes. Social wellbeing and healthy communities are natural outgrowths of individuals practicing and

---

13   Heinlein, Robert A. *Stranger in a Strange Land* / S. Putnam, 1991.

14   Seligman, Martin E. P., and Mihaly Csikszentmihalyi. "Positive Psychology: An Introduction." *Flow and the Foundations of Positive Psychology,* 2014, pp. 279–298., doi:10.1007/978-94-017-9088-8_18.

15   Wood, Alex M., et al. "Gratitude and Well-Being: A Review and Theoretical Integration." *Clinical Psychology Review,* vol. 30, no. 7, 2010, pp. 890–905., doi:10.1016/j.cpr.2010.03.005.

cultivating appreciation. The more people invest, the greater the health of the community.

Remember, the more we notice the details, specifics, and intricacies of others, the more we can truly appreciate them. In times of conflict, we tend to reduce others to labels or caricatures of the truth, so that we can justify our judgments and lack of empathy. By instead remembering to appreciate the depths of people and events, we maintain our power to transform conflict into energy.

AR POWER TOOL
Noticing the Gifts of Others

Simple verbal acknowledgments like "thank you" or "nice job" are only a small part of appreciating others. To create a culture of thriving—not just surviving—it's helpful to begin practicing acknowledgments that are specific, and celebrate the unique "superpowers" of the person they're addressed to.

The next time you want to appreciate someone, try using one of these sentence stems:

What I really appreciate about you is...

What I see you uniquely contributing in the world/to this community is...

The values I see you standing for are...

These types of nuanced and detailed appreciations build connection between individuals, which in turn strengthen the web of community.

When we go through our days on autopilot, we rarely become aware of the efforts others are making all around us. This tool becomes more meaningful the more attentive we are. Listen beyond *what people say*, and start noticing *how they are*. From this vantage point, you'll find plenty worth acknowledging.

Undamning

*The oldest and strongest emotion of mankind is fear,
and the oldest and strongest kind of fear
is fear of the unknown.*

—H.P. LOVECRAFT

As we develop emotional intelligence, we must grapple with the most primal of human emotions: fear. This is the emotion that can most quickly turn our empathy off—especially when we get into a "fight or flight" state.

Here's how it works. In Triune Brain theory, the base of the human brain is sometimes referred to as the "reptilian brain,"[16] as it mimics the form and function of less complicated animal species. This level of our humanity is tied to fear, instinct, and reactivity. It's the control center for our heart rate and other autonomic functions, like regulating our temperature. Because these functions are so vital, the brain stem has the ability to cut us off from our emotions (and the emotions of others) for the sake of our survival. That means when we experience "fight or flight," it can be impossible to access care or understanding.

So, why did our brains develop such a double-edged sword? We are wired to protect ourselves and those closest to us when our survival might be threatened. And often, protection comes in the form of attacking those we see as different or threatening to our group. Unfortunately, we still have this programming

---

16 MacLean, Paul D. *The Triune Brain in Evolution: Role in Paleocerebralfunctions.* Plenum Press, 1990.

when our survival might *not* actually be threatened—causing us to lash out, push away, or otherwise not welcome people into our circle of compassion. Consider xenophobia: the fear of those who are different from us. This phenomenon is the underlying impulse that sparked the Holocaust, and remains the source of racism, discrimination, and much of the war and violence we see in our world.

So, how do we practically combat this? It starts with appreciation.

As humans, we tend to help those we see as similar to ourselves, and to ignore or even disdain those we instinctually and unconsciously categorize as "other." These processes, which have become known as "in-grouping" and "out-grouping,"[17]17 are unconscious and universal. Regardless of how well-intentioned we may be, all of us do this—and it's only when we can *admit* that these protective instincts are part of us that we can consciously enact practices to mitigate their effects. As we gain a greater sense of security in our physical and social worlds, we must continue to broaden the scope of our empathy. In this way, by widening the circle of our "in-group," we can begin to quell our instinctual fears and embody a greater sense of inclusion with those around us.

Authentic Relating has termed this process "undamning." Undamning is the unboxing and un-categorizing of the people (and other beings) with whom we share this planet. The opposite, which we call "boxing," is when we label things in our lives by their surface attributes. It's when we assume we

---

17   Sumner, William Graham. *Folkways: a Study of the Social Importance of Usages, Manners, Customs, Mores, and Morals.* Ginn, 1907.

know what's going on, and don't bother to investigate any further. It is pretty much the opposite of appreciation.

This is our brain's built-in energy conservation process, jumping into action to save our precious processing space. Through this conservation, we can focus on more complex things, with the simpler ones stored away outside of our conscious minds. This is not inherently a "good" or "bad" thing. In fact, it's how both harmful *and* helpful habits are formed.

In this state of mind, however, we're in a kind of auto-pilot—and this is how most of us operate most of the time. Think about how we lump all chairs, stools, couches into the category of "places to sit." We don't need to examine each one to make sure it will support our weight. This saves us time and energy that we can redirect towards more important things, like our colleagues' expectations of us, or tending to the responsibilities of parenting.

Yet while natural and adaptive, there's also a danger to this basic functioning: We can start lumping *people* together. When we engage with thoughts like, "Hispanics are like X," or "Rich white people don't care about Y," we kill curiosity, sever connection, and breed conflict. And as history has shown us, if this process goes too far, the result can be atrocity and genocide.

This is where deep appreciation and "undamning" are vital. It begins with getting curious, and noticing the ways we have put a person or group of people into a box. Consciously removing our labels, and replacing them with curiosity and openness, is the practical application of appreciation.

As we empower each other on the journey toward inclusion, we celebrate and learn from our differences as best we can. For our differences lie in the details, and as we learn to appreciate those details instead of treating others as categories, we begin to rehumanize the people who populate our lives.

The Gratitude Game

Facilitator note: This game takes about 5–10 minutes to play. Setting aside the first few minutes to get centered by breathing slowly and deeply is highly effective for helping people to get the most out of this exercise.

Have participants find a comfortable posture, and enjoy the feeling of being still in mind and body for a few moments. Invite them to notice and appreciate any feelings that come from slowing down.

Next, participants can wander around the room without an agenda, and when ready, let their eyes fall upon any ordinary object. This could be a chair, rug, plant—anything at all. Even something as simple as a pencil or piece of lint will work.

At this stage, participants can begin to bring appreciation to this object in such a way that curiosity, fascination or wonder can be evoked. Some prompts that can be helpful: "As you put all of your senses toward this object, start noticing details that weren't obvious at first glance. Open your mind to feel gratitude for whatever object you have chosen. What can you appreciate? Feel those sensations of gratitude in your body. Now see if you can double the felt sense of appreciation. Now see if you can double it again!"

To go even deeper, have everyone then bring their attention to imagining someone that they love. Some prompts here: "Imagine looking into their eyes, and begin to notice your gratitude for their unique presence in this world. Imagine all the actions and efforts of that person's ancestors that led to this person's being in the world, and in your life today."

Have everyone bring their attention back to their heart, and any felt sensation of gratitude in their body. Ask participants to see if they can find gratitude even for the feeling of gratitude, and to savor this feeling inside. Remind them, if it feels authentic, to give thanks for the joys of being alive, and the ability to experience this form of love.

This is the energy that will grow your heart and your powers of appreciation.

The Noticing Game, which we discussed in the last chapter, helps us get in touch with our inner landscape, so we can extend presence from ourselves to others. In a similar way, The Gratitude Game allows us to magnify our innate goodness and generosity, and extend our care outward in tangible ways. The Gratitude Game exercises our appreciation muscle, just as the Noticing Game exercises our presence muscle.

Yet even when focusing specifically on appreciation, we must start with the present moment. This gives us an access point to the aliveness and juice in our lives: the right now! It's only when we become deeply present with something that we have the opportunity to fully appreciate it, by getting in touch with its details and nuances. This might feel like being startled awake by life's richness!

From here, we'll start to feel our natural curiosity—allowing us to venture into the unknown with joy, rather than struggle. This curiosity is our subject for the next chapter. Presence, appreciation, and curiosity together form the open-hearted exploration of the unknown.

Chapter 7
CURIOSITY

A mind is like a parachute. It only works if it's open.

—Frank Zappa

Curiosity is a guiding force that enriches our social lives, and an ordinary superpower with many benefits. It increases our capacity for lateral (or "out-of-the-box") thinking, and can even help us mend disagreements, as we become more open-minded to the differing viewpoints of others. Choosing to become curious in the face of fear or emotional shutdown is an inherently brave action. It requires that we look at our own uncertainty and admit our limitations. We must face what we don't understand, and choose to respond with open minds and hearts.

Unfortunately, at times we are so dedicated to our beliefs that it can be hard to access curiosity—about ourselves or about others. This is because we all have core beliefs that are closely tied to our identity. When we think of our thoughts and values as *who we are*, it's very difficult to get curious about them. This leads to an obvious question: If we are not our thoughts and values, what are we?

This is a big question and we certainly cannot plumb its depths here, but let's make one point clear. Our identities are not static: They grow organically over time—and sometimes shift dramatically in an instant. If you explore this territory long enough, you might come to the same conclusion as many philosophers and spiritual teachers: We are not our values or what we think, nor are we our name, history, race, or other such traits. Consciousness and identity are malleable and plastic.

The tendency for us humans to constrict tightly around our beliefs is a survival instinct. We cling to certain identities because we are wired to equate our sense of wellbeing with consistency. Thus, when we defend our beliefs, we believe we are defending ourselves. From this vantage point, if someone has, let's say, an opposing political belief, our emotional territory can feel very threatened. In situations like this, we often constrict even further around our belief-narratives. We marshal our defenses, and further, go on the attack to protect ideas and concepts that we hold sacred.

As you can see, there isn't much room for openness and curiosity in this defensive state. So it is our job to strengthen these muscles, especially to prepare us for heated moments. We must investigate our differences like explorers, instead of shielding or attacking like soldiers. Being open to the unknown is necessary to learn anything, but especially to learn from differing viewpoints. And as we're now discovering as a species, the ability for dialogue with those who disagree with us is a key factor in our survival itself.

AR POWER TOOL
Psychological Safety Net

In 2015, Google published research about what makes a productive and innovative team at work.[18] They identified five characteristics, but noted that one of these made all the others possible: psychological safety. Psychological safety is defined as the ability to show and employ one's self without fear of negative consequences of self-image, status or career.[19] It is crucial for people to feel willing to take risks, and for having an authentic culture, where people feel they can be themselves.

Workplaces, like any human or social structure, can be enriching and fulfilling. But many times, the reality is one of unhealthy power dynamics and conflicts that get swept under the rug. Cultures where people feel the need to edit their thoughts and behaviors lead to a diminished sense of freedom—and it doesn't take long before these dynamics kill the creativity of the team as a whole. Unfortunately, this situation isn't uncommon, and has greatly contributed to the surge of interest in improving organizational culture.

As humans operating in any kind of social group or institution, we constantly give each other feedback—whether implicitly or explicitly. There are a myriad of subtle and not-so-subtle ways that we signal approval and disapproval. As the Google

---

18 "Re:Work - The Five Keys to a Successful Google Team." *Google*, Google, rework.with-google.com/blog/five-keys-to-a-successful-google-team/.

19 Kahn, William A. "Psychological Conditions of Personal Engagement and Disengagement at Work." *Academy of Management Journal*, vol. 33, no. 4, 1990, pp. 692–724., doi:10.5465/256287.

study (and many others) have shown, we need effective feedback mechanisms to thrive as a collective. This is uniquely important in the workplace, where our financial survival is on the line.

Safety Statements are one method I have devised for creating psychological safety. This is a way of explicitly and sincerely establishing that we value the relationship, and are committed to staying in connection. When we continually make such commitments (not only in our words, but in our hearts), we transform our environments to allow for more authenticity, curiosity, transparency, creativity, and play. All the good things!

There are two types of Safety Statements: 1) appreciative statements about someone's specific contribution, and 2) validating statements that express what Carl Rogers termed "unconditional positive regard," or basic acceptance and support of a person.[20] Consider the following examples, and how you might personalize them for some of the important people in your life:

You are really important to me. I care about you a lot.

I have your back here.

I want to make sure to get your input on these kinds of things.

It's important to me that you know how valuable you are to this team.

---

20 Rogers, Carl R. "'Client-Centered' Psychotherapy." *Scientific American*, vol. 187, no. 5, 1952, pp. 66–74., doi:10.1038/scientificamerican1152-66.

You Are Not a Thing

Buckminster Fuller, one of my favorite intellectual giants of the 20th century, once famously said, "I seem to be a verb." This quote is a game-changer. The mystery of what we *are* is ultimately unfathomable, but this tiny four-letter word—"verb"—describes the human journey so well.

All our lives, we are trained to think of ourselves as nouns. Just like other nouns, you have a name and a physical substance. Rocks, furniture, books—these are all things. A noun has boundaries and definition. You know what its function is.

The human *being,* on the other hand, is much better described as a process, or a verb. Each day, we take in new sustenance and information, and by the end of the day, we become a new thing! Even if the shifts are subtle, how we define ourselves is in constant flux. And as we will explore in Chapter 8, this constant change takes energy. Growth takes input, and as living beings, we expend significant amounts of energy—even in something as "mundane" as digesting food.

This is why we need to become skillful at harnessing the energy in conflict. Living an authentic life requires that we be *willing to be changed* by our relationships and circumstances. When we practice letting go of our assumptions and expectations, and approach the world instead with openness and curiosity, we begin to see things more as we did when we were children. More freedom becomes available to us, to explore and to celebrate. After all, curiosity is one of the greatest sources of inspiration and vitality we have. We need only observe the boundless energy of children to remember that this is true!

One of the most beautiful fruits of Authentic Relating practice is the reawakening of our childlike curiosity. As children, we are highly impressionable—and while this means we're more vulnerable, it also means we're more receptive. In our early years, we are still forming our self-identities. We take in thousands of impressions every day, and that receptivity forms the foundation of our future capacities and ways of being in relationship.

As we age, we become less impressionable, which is to say, more self-defined. Our personal values and beliefs about the world around us (and the worlds inside us) come into sharper definition, and we begin to mistake this definition for *who we are.* Of course, it's healthy to have a clear sense of self—but is also healthy to have a clear sense of "not knowing." This balance point between self-definition and self-exploration is also, in a way, the balance point between *dignity* and *humility*: Dignity is the ability to "Know Thyself" like Socrates, and humility is our capacity to be "open" like Zappa's parachute.

The deeper we investigate our self-imposed identities, the more we'll discover of the boundaries and defenses that keep our internal conditions stable. Think of our personality's defenses as the membrane of a cell: Some things get in, and others are blocked—for good reason. If our internal psychology is disrupted too intensely or too quickly, it can destabilize our mental health. Yet in order to learn anything, we *must* allow novel information to enter, and allow ourselves to be changed by it. It's a wonderfully sticky catch-22.

The solution lies in applying an understanding of ourselves as verbs instead of nouns. When our identity becomes the process of growth *itself*, instead of a static entity, we can begin to truly embody the superpower of curiosity.

AR POWER TOOL
Artful Interruption

We have all experienced the heart's ability to guide us, compass-like, toward things that feel alive, energy-giving, and exciting. We've also experienced it shut down and retract, away from those things that feel boring or deadening. And we've all, no doubt, had both of these experiences in conversations with people.

The good news is that conversations, in and of themselves, are not inherently boring or exciting. In fact, we can actually train ourselves to infuse more energy into our connections through the ordinary super power of curiosity. So the next time you find yourself feeling bored in a conversation, instead of politely tolerating, try this:

Be on the lookout for that ping of aliveness, even if it is small, when the other person is talking. What are you curious about? What feels interesting here? When you find it, interrupt! When we can sincerely find one thing that is even mildly intriguing, we can steer ourselves toward something that is more enjoyable for both parties. For example, you might say, *How did it affect you when she said that?* or, *Why did you get into that in the first place?* This is a great way to get out of the informational mode of communication and into the personal.

You can also simply ask, *Why is this important to you?* This can bring us out of autopilot, and nudge us to explore deeper. In this way, the conversation itself can also find more depth. Next time you find yourself in a boring conversation, instead of immediately looking for the exit, try taking social leadership through an artful interruption.

The Curiosity Game

The Curiosity Game is one the most foundational of all AR Games, and a staple in many Games Nights and workshops. Seen through the kaleidoscope of our deepest curiosity, anything or anyone is magical. The goal of this game is to unlock this radical curiosity, and we do this by letting go of what we think we "should" be asking about, in service of finding the topics we are really curious about in the moment with this specific person. Remember, when we get *interested*, people become *interesting*.

Despite its simplicity, this game has been known to reliably produce beautiful and rich conversation within a matter of minutes. How? We mix our childlike impulses to play and explore, with the richness of all the experiences we've accumulated as adults.

As previously mentioned, Curiosity couples well with the Power Tool of Artful Interruption, which encourages us to include our own desires in an exchange. In this game, a vital component is *interrupting* the person answering with a polite "thank you," once we feel complete on a topic. This helps keep the questioner engaged, and firmly in the driver's seat. Curiosity is continuously fueling the conversation.

To begin, have everyone find a partner. Partner A will be the first person *asking* questions; Partner B will be answering them. Once the round is completed, participants will switch roles.

In Round 1, Partner A has 3–5 minutes to ask Partner B any questions they want. Questions should come from a place of genuine curiosity. You might prompt participants to notice, "What are your automatic, go-to questions—the ones you think you 'should' ask? And what comes up when you let your real curiosity speak—the thing you might think you 'can't' ask?" There are no limits and no rules around the questions, though Partner B is equally free to decline or respond to questions how they wish.

Round 2 is an opportunity for the answerer to give feedback—something we rarely get in an ordinary conversation! For 1–2 minutes, Partner A continues with questions, but this time Partner B gives feedback in lieu of answers, holding up one to five fingers to indicate their feelings about the question. One finger means, "That question is boring or a turnoff. I'm looking for the exit in this conversation." At the other end of the spectrum, five fingers means, "I can hardly wait to answer it!" For this round, Partner B does not give any actual answers, only hand signals.

During Round 3, Partner A is now equipped with more information about Partner B, and should hold the intention of keeping the conversation engaging and lively. For another 3–5 minutes, Partner A continues questioning, using the feedback given as they choose. As in Round 1, Partner A should continue to practice following their aliveness, and Partner B should continue to practice honouring their own boundaries—maintaining both curiosity and social safety, while keeping the conversation moving.

Finally, with Round 4, the two partners come to a completion, with 2–4 minutes allotted for sharing impact. This is perhaps the truest gift of our time and attention. Partner A will complete the following sentence stems for Partner B: "The moment I felt you the most was..." and "What I think I'm starting to get about you is..."

With this round complete, the two participants can switch roles and repeat the process.

Chapter 8
HOLOGRAM

---

*The world is a holographic universe, with every piece
containing the whole.*

—MARIANNE WILLIAMSON

So far, we have investigated how the qualities of presence, appreciation, and curiosity can powerfully accelerate our growth and emotional awareness. The previous chapters have prepared us for perhaps the most transformative aspect of Authentic Relating practice: the concept of the *personal hologram.*

Our "hologram" is the lens through which we experience and make meaning of the world. It is unique to every one of us, yet ubiquitous across our lives. As the old adage goes, *The way we do one thing is the way we do everything.* Thus, when we begin to perceive our hologram and to work directly with it, powerful change can happen remarkably quickly.

Another way to look at the hologram is as a fully three-dimensional picture, giving us a full view of something in its entirety from any angle. If a picture is worth a thousand words, a hologram is worth a million. Yet in Authentic Relating terms, "seeing our hologram" means much more than simply seeing the details of ourselves. It means welcoming each detail as both valid in its own right, revealing and ultimately transforming the parts that aren't serving us. Through this process, we become more aware, awake, and whole.

When we glimpse our personal hologram and then come to understand it, we become tapped into massive potential for rapid growth. This backward step is akin to seeing our own eyeballs, or being able to "bend" The Matrix. One of the great powers of Authentic Relating practice is this revelation of our relational blind spots. Each of us is limited in what we can perceive, and we need each other to be able to clearly see ourselves. Community is the primary resource we have for waking up to, integrating, and beginning to free ourselves from the past relational limitations we were not consciously aware of.

A clear insight into one's hologram can feel like a lightning bolt. These epiphanies can show us the internal patterns that have been shaping our entire lives. Often, we discover patterns that have been directing the course of our relationships for years and even decades—hidden in plain sight. These realizations, however humbling they may be, are in fact an opportunity to radically change our relational habits for the better. The more we incorporate Authentic Relating practice into our everyday lives, the more of these "lighting strikes" we can experience.

AR POWER TOOL
Invite Feedback

Inviting feedback from others initiates feedback loops of emotional learning, in which we become aware of how we are affecting someone, and this knowledge creates more choice for how we show up in connection. When we commit to this process with people we trust, it builds intimacy and closeness as well.

Requesting and receiving feedback about our performance on a specific task is one layer that can be helpful. But if we want to truly grow, we can take this further by inviting feedback on how others *feel* in our presence. This type of feedback is rare, and understandably so: Exposing ourselves to outside opinions can feel extremely vulnerable. This is why it's important to begin this practice with people you feel safe around, and who can give feedback in a way that you are willing and able to receive. This tool is not meant to feed self-judgment or shame—quite the opposite. After all, we can only bring curiosity and acceptance to what we can see.

Sample phrases to invite feedback:

I want us to have the type of relationship where we can share important things with each other, even if they're uncomfortable. Is there anything you haven't shared with me that might help us feel closer?

How would you feel about giving each other some feedback every time we finish a project together? This could help us work with each other better in the future.

Remember, it's important to take ample time to fully understand each person's needs around feedback, to create psychological safety. So be sure to do this at a time when both parties are feeling resourced and relaxed.

The Climate for Lightning to Strike

Be yourself. The universe will give you feedback.

—RAM DASS

One of the unique facets of Authentic Relating is that it catalyzes growth through relationship, rather than as an individual undertaking. We need each other to thrive—and the intimacy of our relationships is actually the best accelerant for effective personal development. This orientation is directly in opposition to the rugged individualism that has been the hallmark of Western culture. Simply put, it's an acknowledgment that we need each other, and that this dependency is actually a good thing.

Within its community of practitioners, the Authentic Relating movement strives to create a web of relationships that exist in the balance point between acceptance and growth. Practicing radical acceptance of others, while still maintaining our ability to speak our truth and ask for what we need, are both key to fostering a resilient group culture. Rather than either orientation on its own, it is this "both/and" that brings the potency.

In AR, we start exactly as we are, where we are—with full acceptance of our limitations. Yet we must also be willing to shine a light on the unhelpful relationship patterns and programs we've accumulated, and to receive and integrate others' feedback with grace. With dignity and humility in balance, we can receive feedback more comfortably and consider it objectively—without responding reactively, or accepting it as absolute truth.

When we are in community, there will always be moments when we rub each other the wrong way. We may sense people approving of or judging us, but not know if our impressions are correct. This social feedback is often subtle, unspoken, or difficult to interpret. Authentic Relating presents a model of feedback that can be both kind and direct. Through practicing AR, we learn to give, receive, and *invite* feedback more skillfully, with presence, empathy, and transparency at the same time.

A healthy community is one in which a diversity of perspectives can be welcomed and integrated. The more this process occurs, the more growth and learning is possible for each individual. These feedback loops develop quickly in communities of AR practitioners because of the sheer variety of perspectives being exchanged and considered with empathy. Where one-on-one relationships can be powerful mirrors, communities can reveal us to ourselves in three dimensions. Thus, this is where the capacity to see our personal hologram is best developed—and where "lightning" can most easily strike.

Creating Change that Lasts

Until now, we've been discussing many elements that can bring about great change in your life. You have many tools, know the importance of authentic community, and have learned about seeing yourself in three dimensions (your "hologram"). If you're already implementing the practices and lessons so far, you may already be witnessing changes taking place in your life.

How can we make such changes last? We must first remember that *we* are ever-changing; we are not nouns, but verbs. And in order to keep changing and growing in the right direction, a lot of energy is required. This is why community—or our "tribe"—is so important. Just as community can create the conditions for those brief flashes of lightning, it can also help establish the foundations necessary for long-lasting change.

A sense of community, for one thing, is powerful in reducing our fear—and the more afraid we are, the less access we have to our higher values and ways of being. In the ancient past, our ancestors worried about food availability and animal attacks. Today, we worry more about connection and belonging. Finding our "tribe," and maintaining healthy communities, are skills we must develop for our nervous systems to feel safe. This frees the higher capacities of our hearts and our minds to come forward.

When our core human need to belong is met in healthy ways, the effects are profound. We are more likely to push our own edges of vulnerability, and to be willing to receive feedback on how our behavior and words affect others. As a result, our fear is lessened, and our higher intentions more easefully embodied.

Integration Ingredients

Have you ever baked cookies and then eaten them straight out of the oven? Beyond burning your tongue, they probably fell apart in a gooey mess. Just like freshly baked cookies, our experiences and insights need time and space to consolidate. That's why planning for integration time is important for our development. To think about this another way, consider sleep. Adults do best with 7–8 hours of sleep every night. Teenagers need 9–10 hours and new infants can sleep as much as 18 hours a day! The more rapidly we are changing, the more rest and downtime is needed to integrate the change.

The insights that come from becoming aware of our hologram offer us a powerful opportunity to "reorganize" ourselves at a higher level of development. While this may be a wonderful upgrade, it begins with a disruption to our sense of self. Like those freshly baked cookies, we need uninterrupted "counter time" to solidify and settle into our new form.

Our nervous systems process and integrate change in a complex manner. For most people, movement, rest, and touch are essential ingredients for integration. Many of us also need time in solitude, though every person's integration process is unique. However it looks, with this kind of transformational work, self-care is not a luxury, but a necessity.

Part III
TRANSFORMING CONFLICT

Living an Authentic Life

By definition, the courageous conversation is the one you are not having now, and the one you don't want to have.

—DAVID WHYTE

Understandably, we often shy away from authentic conversations. Broaching subjects that require deep honesty can be mentally and emotionally taxing—not to mention scary if we're not used to such vulnerability. As a society, we simply haven't learned the tools for navigating this territory, in the same way we've learned to write an essay or make spreadsheets. Luckily, if you're reading this book, you're already ahead of the curve.

As a movement, we envision a world where emotional education is as ubiquitous as math and science class or physical education. Just as we must exercise our minds and our bodies, we must also train our hearts if we are to thrive in today's world. We must learn how to make sense of our emotions, come to wise relational decisions, and develop our intuition—and we must do this in a way that can honor and hold our individual differences. In our increasingly complex world, these are the foundations from which we can chart a course toward harmony.

In this section, we'll discuss the transformation of conflict. While there will be a focus on organizational and group conflict, these skills can apply just as readily to conflict within our personal relationships—and to our relationships as a whole. This transformational process has several important ingredients: setting context, using our "Jedi senses," and the two conflict transformation tools of *Emotional Alchemy* and *Emotional Aikido*. Though these are some of the more difficult-to-master skills in this book, with all of the information and tools you have learned so far, you will be well-equipped. Learning these skills can be a catalyst for exponential relational growth—and for unlocking enormous energy reserves in your life.

Chapter 9
CONTEXT

The three great mysteries:
A bird unto air, a fish unto water,
a man unto himself

—ANONYMOUS

Context is ubiquitous: It *is* the water we collectively swim in. In this sense, it's something of a miracle that we can become aware of our context at all. Yet indeed, there are moments we *feel* the air around us—and realize, viscerally, that we have emerged from the water. From this place, the possibility opens up to venture into a new world. Learning to be "context-aware" gives us access to our deepest creationary power, where we can become culture-*creators* instead of blindly following the flow. Just like our earliest ancestors made the leap from ocean to land, so too does this potential exist for us all the time. But just like our ancestors, this is no easy feat. For our formerly aquatic friends, the "leap" took 30 million years.[21]

---

21 Maciver, Malcolm A., et al. "Massive Increase in Visual Range Preceded the Origin of Terrestrial Vertebrates." *Proceedings of the National Academy of Sciences*, vol. 114, no. 12, 2017, doi:10.1073/pnas.1615563114.

"Context," in its pervasiveness, can be an elusive term. One simple way to look at context is a set of implicit (unspoken) agreements we make. Right now, for instance, one element of our context is that this book is written in English. If I suddenly switched to Latin, our implicit agreement would be broken. Let's remain in English for the rest of the book, shall we? Now, our agreement is explicit.

How could something so absurdly obvious be useful? Well, the context we live in literally creates all the possibilities and limitations for the quality of our lives. *Setting context* is the swiss army knife of AR because it applies to nearly every life situation. This makes sense, if you look at the dictionary definition of the word: "The circumstances that form the setting for an event, statement, or idea, and in terms of which it can be fully understood and assessed." By setting context, we can literally shape the fundamental fabric that surrounds us.

When we do the work to set context with others, we help the group as a whole become more integrated and cohesive. This is an act that teachers and leaders (and parents!) know can take a lot of emotional energy. In its most basic form, this can be a statement about what's happening, or about to happen. Sometimes it looks as simple as, "Just so you know when you walked in, we were discussing the current political situation." By making a statement like this, we are helping another integrate into the situation with minimal confusion.

Of course, setting context can be much more complex. Often when two people disagree, the conflict has originated from mismatching contexts. Consider how, for example, the word "soon" is entirely subjective. For one person in the interaction, it may mean a few hours; for the other, it may mean a few weeks. Each may be clear in their own understanding, while completely oblivious to the other's. This is where the practice of *Assume Nothing* can really come in handy!

Noticing and naming the unspoken context is sometimes all that's needed for untangling these misunderstandings. While it's possible to do this once conflict has already arisen, life becomes so much easier when we learn to do this *before* we are in conflict. Often, this looks like getting shared reality around expectations from the outset.

Shaping Culture

Every business, organization, and pair of people has a culture. And even though we cannot see them with our eyes, these cultures can feel concrete. Think of the "culture" of two best friends who can complete each other's sentences. Such cultures are the result of many small interactions over time, eventually creating something quite sturdy.

The longer a group has been together, the more difficult the culture can be to shift—though understanding this simple truth is the first step in doing so. If we can become conscious of the existing context, eventually we can change it. We can even create new ones, becoming "culture creators" and designers.

We can infer four different types of context from the definition referenced earlier: physical, structural, psychological/emotional, and visionary. Masterfully setting each of these can create shifts on both the individual and organizational level. Let's take a closer look at each.

Physical Context, or The Possibilities and Limitations Set by Objects and Space

At one level, context is strictly the physical setting in which something happens. Generally, people don't question a simple context like the layout of a room; we naturally flow into and follow the context that existed before we arrived, usually unconsciously. If chairs are set up in a circle, for example, people will typically sit in them in the way they were arranged.

Any aspect of a physical space that can be perceived by the senses is part of the physical context. One way we can increase our awareness of this domain is simply to put our attention and curiosity on the design and layout of a space. For example: How do you feel in a room with low ceilings versus a room with vaulted ceilings? How do you feel in a room that is painted yellow versus one that is painted red?

Of course, not all physical context is designed by humans. Things like the weather, terrain, or whether it's daytime or night, are also examples of physical context. In any case, becoming aware of these elements and how they affect us is to become aware of our physical context.

AR POWER TOOL
Changing Configuration

Next time you're in a tense or emotionally charged inter-action, try simply switching locations or another element of the physical context. This might mean sitting versus stand-ing, going to a more private space, getting some air, or sit-ting beside rather than across from each other. Of course, be sure to make the invitation with intelligent attunement. For example, rather than interrupting with, *Let's move,* you might ask, *What if we moved to a space that's more comfort-able to talk?*

When facilitating a group, simply inviting everyone to come closer can palpably shift the dynamic. Sometimes this looks like forming a "better" circle: one that is rounder, where everyone can more easily see everyone else. This type of sug-gestion can also be a reminder of how we often feel the effects of physical context without realizing it. Or, that we might real-ize it and say nothing, unconsciously expecting the leader to make any necessary adjustments.

As AR practitioners, we can be social and cultural lead-ers wherever we go—even if we are new to the group, or not explicitly in a leadership role. In our awareness of context and our willingness to speak up and shift it, we *become* leaders, regardless of the situation.

Structural Context, or Laying Out the Blueprint

As we've all experienced, misunderstandings often occur when our communication is taken out of context. Perhaps someone didn't hear the first part of our conversation. Perhaps we have some confusion going on internally that makes our communication difficult to understand. Or perhaps, we forgot to state our intention before we went on to share some challenging feedback.

Think of it like this: When we only have one or two puzzle pieces, it's impossible to get a sense of the picture as a whole. Creating a clearer structural context is like bringing in new "puzzle pieces" of information. All of these add up to a more holistic understanding than would be possible looking at any piece on its own.

Another concrete example of structural context is the college term paper: The opening and closing paragraphs (the thesis statement and conclusion) *create structure* for the rest of the paper. Without knowing the main idea, a reader couldn't properly interpret all the details, and would likely feel lost and disconnected from the topic. The main ideas stated upfront contextualize what's in the middle. The conclusion at the end reinforces the themes in a way that gives context to all the evidence again.

As you can see, the structure (which includes the order in which we choose to share information) can help others to more accurately understand us. And this is equally applicable for real-life conversations. After all, no one else is inside our head! In "laying out the blueprint" for our conversations in the first place, everything that follows is more easily interpretable and clear. This practice is especially important when we find ourselves in challenging situations that have a significant impact on our relationships.

AR POWER TOOL
Saved by Context

From time to time, everyone puts their foot in their mouth. This tool is designed to help remove that foot—to "save" those moments where we lacked skill in our communication.

Imagine: You are sharing something emotional with a friend, and their face is taking on an expression of confusion and hurt. Stop and rewind to the context. You might say:

I notice that you look hurt, and want to reassure you that I'm not mad or trying to criticize you. I'm saying all this in the hopes that next time we can communicate more effectively and efficiently, because our friendship is really important to me.

Context is always valuable, even if set in the middle of an interaction. The friend who may have felt defensive or hurt just a moment before is now being enlisted in helping sustain a meaningful friendship. Once others are clearer around our intentions, they will likely relax their defenses. In this way, we can "rescue" our interactions using context, and create more mutual understanding.

Psychological/Emotional Context, or Our Energetic Impact on Others

Our attitude, body language, tone of voice, and energy levels all impact how our communication is received by others. Explained another way, even when we aren't intentionally setting context, our *embodiment* communicates nonverbal context to others—whether we're aware of it or not.

To embark on the path of Authentic Relating is to commit to becoming more conscious of our emotional and psychological context. There is great power in this awareness: As we notice the contexts we "give off" to others, we can begin to have a more intentional impact on our relationships and communities. Like it or not, we are always influencing the culture around us. The more aware we are, the more we can *choose* the influence we want to have.

As we saw in the opening of this chapter, the ability to set context and shape culture is a hallmark of leadership— and also a responsibility. Without clear facilitation and direction, the tendency for a group will be to return to the status quo. This can mean a default towards self-protectiveness. For example, in company culture, if there is an air of dissatisfaction and complaining, leaders must address this by setting a new cultural context, or productivity will be hampered by the lack of good morale. Said another way, our attitudes and emotions are powerful and contagious, and a good leader wields this power consciously.

AR POWER TOOL
Noticing Mindset,
or "What game am I playing?"

In personal-growth literature, psychological context is often described as our "mindset," and the idea of "changing our mindset" is pervasive. Of course, if we're unaware of the beliefs layered deep in our unconscious, changing our conscious mind will simply be a bandaid. In other words, the first step to changing anything must be to notice it— to become what we call "context-aware." One way of developing this awareness is to notice the language we use. Try picking a topic or a theme, and pay special attention whenever you hear yourself talk about it—as if it wasn't even you, but someone else you're overhearing. You can even pretend you're a spy, and that it's your job to listen closely for important information and clues.

One powerful example is to notice your mindset around time. Maybe you hear yourself saying things like, *I'm so busy!* or, *I don't have time!* or, *I'm sorry I'm late again. I'm bad at keeping track of time.* Gradually, you might realize your mindset is generally "stressed" around time

In this exercise, we are exercising our muscle of context-awareness. As we train ourselves in making our implicit mindsets explicit, we can begin to see how deeply our unexamined beliefs affect our lives. To advance this tool, try asking the question: "What game am I playing?" or "What unspoken agreements might I be following?" This inquiry can help us wake up to how we shape the cultures we're in, ultimately leading us to greater empowerment.

Visionary Context, or Our Desired Future Outcome

Learning to set visionary context is a vital skill for creating change at the societal level. The more trusted and coherent our leadership is, the more likely others will join and follow us—and this is often directly related to our ability to set visionary context. The leaders we admire often have a magnetic and magnanimous quality. If we remember our study of activating the energy of our hearts in Chapter 6 (through the power of appreciation), it is easy to see why. The heart generates an electromagnetic field that can deeply affect others. This process is sometimes called enrollment, or getting buy-in from others (which we will discuss in greater detail later on in this chapter).

There are three important steps in setting any context: noticing, naming, and offering. First we must notice what the current context is, i.e. become context-aware. Then, we must have the courage to name it explicitly. And finally, we must have a new and better context to offer.

We can see a beautiful example of embodied, visionary context in the work of Dr. Martin Luther King, Jr. He saw that the existing context of segregation and Jim Crow laws in 1960s America were not only unjust, but detrimental to the health of the society as a whole. Meanwhile, others saw these conditions as simple facts of life, because it was the context in which they were born and raised. But Dr. King (and other civil rights leaders) continued to notice and name the problematic context, and to courageously offer a new possibility.

In what is now one of the most famous speeches in history, King perfectly exemplifies what it is to notice, name, and offer a new, visionary context:

> *Five score years ago, a great American, in whose symbolic shadow we stand today, signed the Emancipation Proclamation. This momentous decree came as a great beacon of light of hope to millions of Negro slaves who had been seared in the flames of withering injustice. It came as a joyous daybreak to end the long night of their captivity.*

> *But one hundred years later, the Negro still is not free. One hundred years later, the life of the Negro is still sadly crippled by the manacles of segregation and the chains of discrimination. One hundred years later, the Negro lives on a lonely island of poverty in the midst of a vast ocean of material prosperity. One hundred years later, the Negro is still languishing in the corners of American society and finds himself an exile in his own land.*

> *I have a dream that one day this nation will rise up and live out the true meaning of its creed: "We hold these truths to be self-evident: that all men are created equal."*

> *I have a dream that one day on the red hills of Georgia the sons of former slaves and the sons of former slave owners will be able to sit down together at the table of brotherhood.*

> *I have a dream that one day even the state of Mississippi, a state sweltering with the heat of injustice, sweltering with*

the heat of oppression, will be transformed into an oasis of freedom and justice.

I have a dream that my four little children will one day live in a nation where they will not be judged by the color of their skin but by the content of their character. From every mountainside, let freedom ring.

And when this happens, and when we allow freedom to ring, when we let it ring from every village and every hamlet, from every state and every city, we will be able to speed up that day when all of God's children, black men and white men, Jews and gentiles, Protestants and Catholics, will be able to join hands and sing in the words of the old Negro spiritual, "Free at last! Free at last! Thank God Almighty, we are free at last!"[22]

Setting Context Steps

Reading this profound speech allows us to see the structure of offering a well-received visionary context. Dr. King repeatedly names the existing context, then offers something inspiring based on his own personal values in the world he wants to live in. The powerful effects of such context-setting remain evident decades later.

Setting context is the primary tool we have to create more of what we want in the world. The formula to remember when we are setting context in our lives is *notice, name, offer.*

---

22   King, Martin L., Jr. "I Have a Dream." Speech. Lincoln Memorial, Washington, D. C. 28 Aug. 1963. American Rhetoric. Web. 25 Mar. 2013.

Step #1: Notice the context

This is the moment we wake up to the water we are swimming in, and the first step in becoming a leader who sees subtle patterns and dynamics that others don't or won't. Recall what it was like when we noticed our unspoken "deal" to speak English. Where else in your life might you be making unconscious "agreements"?

Step #2: Name the context with others

Have the courage to speak aloud the things you notice are happening underneath the surface. In many social situations, this may involve pointing to the existing context in a way that is non-judgmental. If people feel defensive, the necessary fertile ground for Step 3 will not be created.

Step #3: Offer a new context

Paint a picture of what is possible: of a world that has more of what you value in it. These offerings of new context open the doors to create the world we want to live in. Using visual language is often helpful, and can invite others to co-create with you. Examples: "I'm imagining that we would…" "I'm picturing the type of evening where we…" "If we run the project this way, I'm imagining we would all feel…"

AR POWER TOOL
Headline – Consent

As we have been exploring in this chapter, the capacity to set context is a form of leadership—and this type of relational leadership is a quality we can bring into our everyday lives. Setting context doesn't need to be a big undertaking. We can do it in small ways, honing our leadership and communication at the same time.

A simple tool for setting context is to start with a "headline," and then ask for consent from the other. In this way, you can introduce "bite-sized" opportunities for course-corrections in your relationships. The "headline" is a statement, and the "consent" is a question.

Here are some examples:

I want to share something on a different topic. Are you open to changing subjects?

I want to be heard around something challenging happening in my life right now. Are you available to listen?

This conversation is important for me, and I want to go slow. Can we start with a little synced breathing and eye contact to get connected?

Something that is happening right now doesn't feel good to me. Can we take a moment to get curious about it?

The Power of Enrollment

As mentioned earlier, understanding context is necessary to enroll others in your vision. And whether your vision is of changing the world for the better or hosting an epic dinner party, the principles of enrolling others are the same.

First of all, we must be aware and present in order to perceive whether or not our communication is attuned to another person. If we notice how our communication is being received in real time, we will be far more effective in enrolling others in our vision. Remember, tuning into the relational field between ourselves and others is a muscle we can develop simply by practicing often.

Second, we must harness our excitement, passion, and energy, to draw people into our vision. This points to the importance of body language and tone of voice, especially when we are inviting others into something that requires a significant time or energy commitment. Of course, this is not a "performance" of persuasion, but a practice of revealing ourselves vulnerably. When we offer ourselves nakedly in this way, we are more accessible and others feel more drawn-in.

Third, we must recognize and accept that humans naturally consider themselves first. Upon hearing a new proposal, people generally ask themselves, "Is this feasible?" and "Does this benefit me?" Knowing this about human nature, it can be helpful to create scenarios that others can imagine. In other words, it must be clear how others can plug into your vision in practical and beneficial ways. People often think in terms of pictures and will need to be able to imagine themselves playing a role that they feel good about. If you are attempting to enroll someone, doing this "illustration" for them can easily be the deciding factor.

If you can answer the questions, "What's in it for you?" *and* "What's in it for me?" you are well ahead of the curve in setting powerful context. Notice how this is a form of the fifth practice in action (*Honor Self and Other*). While it's important to demonstrate the ways our proposal is of service to the other, it's also important to acknowledge our own interests. When we are transparent about our motivations, we mitigate potential suspicion, and get the chance to share our deeper "why." In fact, these two outcomes are inextricable: The more of ourselves we reveal, the more trust others tend to feel. This is why our hopes or intentions are often the most powerful piece of context. If the person you're trying to persuade resonates with your motivations, they are much more likely to help—and at the core, all of our motivations come down to the same universal human needs.

Chapter 10
LISTENING

---

*The single biggest problem in communication
is the illusion that it has taken place.*

—George Bernard Shaw

A core tenant of AR is the belief that listening can begin to heal any conflict. Deep embodied listening is not passive but creative and generative. By truly listening, we add energy and awareness to a situation.

The act of true and complete listening serves to link people's nervous systems together, and as a result, two significant things happen. First, rich emotional energy and information gets exchanged because we are in resonance. The learning that results from this exchange allows us to handle greater and greater levels of complexity in our communication and relationships. Second, through this linking of our hearts with deep embodied listening, we become capable of processing vast amounts of emotional energy. The increase in capacity is nearly exponential. When two people are truly listening to each other, 1+1 = 11!

Unfortunately, if we haven't been specifically trained in this advanced form of listening, we may have picked up the cultural defaults that so many of us are handed. Typically, the way we listen (and even what we hear) is based on our own cultural lens and personal history. We don't see or hear objectively. Each of us sees and hears through our own individual hologram. Of course, Authentic Relating is not about learning to be completely objective. It's about bringing awareness, agency, and embodiment to our deeply subjective truths.

Our attachment to particular outcomes can also color the picture. Yet, our attachments and desires are a natural part of us. Trying to simply erase them would be ceasing to honor ourselves—not to mention impossible. Instead, just naming or acknowledging these "agendas" (whether internally or out loud) can bring us back to the present moment: the only place where true listening can occur.

True listening is selfless in the sense that we refrain, as best as we are able, from filtering communication through our beliefs or perceptions, which may be distorted. With this more fully-embodied listening, we loosen our grip on any assumptions, and give our full attention to what we are experiencing at *this* moment. This goes far beyond a person's speech. We often say in AR, "Communication happens when I hear your heart." In this place, we *feel* the intent beneath the words.

The way to achieve this is to slow down and get present. Much of what you have learned so far in this book will help you here: the willingness to welcome, check our assumptions, and honor the experience of both parties. These skills combined add up to what I like to call "Jedi Listening": another ordinary superpower.

"Jedi Listening" creates a feeling of immediacy and aliveness. It is a doorway into the here and now. With this practice, the relational energy between people becomes palpable in a way that can feel electric. Where assumptions and expectations close doors, true listening opens a universe between us.

AR POWER TOOL
What's Underneath?

Human rights activist turned filmmaker Deeyah Khan makes gut-wrenching documentaries about extremists like jihadists and neo-nazis.[23,24] Rather than depicting these individuals as monsters, Khan's films have a way of revealing the scared child beneath the surface, ultimately giving rise to their acts of emotional hardness and hate. In essence, Khan is a master at asking the question, *What's underneath?*

When we speak, there is always the surface and the underbelly. Sometimes this underbelly is referred to as "subtext." Asking, *What's underneath?* can allow us to cut through confusing situations or create more depth.

The aim here is to go deeper in a way that is appropriate to the situation. Usually, we're dealing with a complaining friend, as opposed to a neo-nazi! In any case, if we interrupt too soon, we may be bypassing an essential step of listening. Once a person feels heard, we can then move to asking about their values, desires, and needs (e.g., *What do you think you need in this situation?*).

Or if a partner is sharing about a change in attitude of where the couple should live, for example we could ask: *What might that mean for us?* or, *Can we dream about this together?*

---

23   Khan, Deeyah. "Jihad: A Story of Others." *YouTube,* uploaded by Fuuse. 14 Aug. 2016. https://youtu.be/_usgevtEppg.

24   Khan, Deeyah. "White Right: Meeting the Enemy." *TVO Documentaries,* 28 Feb. 2020. https://www.tvo.org/video/documentaries/white-right-meeting-the-enemy.

This directs the conversation to more connection and more of a relational space.

Listening as a Bridge of Connection

John Gottman is a living legend in the field of interpersonal relationships. For decades, he and his team at the Gottman Institute have been researching healthy communication in relationships. The institute has developed a formula with 90% accuracy(!) for predicting whether a married couple will divorce.[25]

This extensive research into romantic partnership has a lot to teach us about *all* relationships. In 30 years of research, one of the most important conclusions is this: *Listening to one another is the most powerful tool we have.* Through training, we can eventually become able to hear each other's intentions, even when they aren't communicated directly. This is especially important in times of tension and disconnection—inevitabilities in any relationship. Couples (or any group of people) who practice this vital skill are consistently better able to navigate the challenges of life together.

Authentic Relating has an advanced curriculum on the topic of listening that builds upon some of these basic insights from Gottman. My definition of Jedi Listening has five layers: listening to *reply, understand, empathize, mentor,* and *appreciate fully.* When we are highly present and "tuned in," we can listen at all five layers simultaneously. Let's take a closer look at each.

---

25   Gottman, John, and Nan Silver. *Why Marriages Succeed or Fail.* Bloomsbury Paperbacks, 2014.

Listening with the Intent to Reply

This is likely our default before we discover practices like Authentic Relating. It is a state of being on autopilot: already thinking of the next thing we want to say while the other is still speaking. This isn't always a bad thing—in some situations, this type of listening can be necessary or helpful.

In many professional environments, for example, the best ideas often come from a combination of many people's thoughts. When there is a faster pace of conversation, listening with the intent to reply is simply functional. This rapid exchange of opinions—as long as there is psychological safety—can leverage diversity to generate creative new ideas, and to improve everyone's thinking in a situation. Exploring these ideas in more depth can then follow.

In other words, it can make sense to listen with the intent to reply, *if* the aim is to help people make better decisions and to think more critically. When I'm in this mode of listening, my focus isn't even necessarily on you, but on my own thoughts.

Of course, listening with the intent to reply becomes unhelpful when it becomes our default mode. Many of us go through much of our interactions implicitly assuming that the other person *wants* to hear our thoughts, whether or not they made this request. Sometimes this can kill any possibility for connection on the spot. The person talking doesn't feel received or heard, and the conversation fizzles out in the absence of a sense of "we."

Often being on the receiving end of this type of listening can feel like a rejection, and repeated over time, this can do significant damage to our relationships. So the next time you notice that you're in this mode with someone, try pausing before responding. Instead of immediately jumping in, you might try first paraphrasing what you've heard. And if you want to share an opinion, first check: "Do you want to hear my thoughts on this?"

Listening with the Intent to Understand

Listening with the intent to understand means we are committed to creating "shared reality." Shared reality is when we are both confident that we're on the same page—that we have mutual understanding. You are clear about something I have expressed, and I know that you are clear because you have said it back to me accurately. If it sounds circular, it is!

This type of listening means that we are tracking both verbal and nonverbal communication, in an earnest attempt to understand its full meaning and implications. In order to get into this listening mode, we need to have come out of the first mode (listening to reply). This second mode has a feeling of patience and respect to it, and for a serious AR practitioner, becomes a natural response to disagreement and misunderstanding. In this way, we can often prevent hurt before it even occurs.

AR *MASTER* TOOL
Reflective Listening

This is a tool often overlooked for its sheer simplicity. To use it, listen to the speaker without interruption. When they are finished speaking, reflect back to them what they just said. As best you can, try to summarize *without interpretation, advice-giving, or an agenda.* You can even begin with the words, "What I heard you say is…"

This allows the speaker an experience of feeling deeply seen and heard, and can also act as an invitation for them to share more. Though it can work at any time, this tool is at its most powerful during conflict. When someone is upset or frustrated, reflecting their words and letting them know you want to hear them fully can have the emotional effect of defusing a ticking bomb.

I call this one a *Master* Tool because of its incredible versatility. Sometimes even reflecting a single word or a phrase can foster safety that inspires further sharing. Our reflections signal our engagement with others' words, and can build energy in a conversation.

Taking the time to build these foundations creates a territory of connection, friendship, and bonding. Whether our shared reality is intellectual, emotional, or philosophical, we build it layer by layer, through our listening and reflection. (See page 190 for the empathy game which teaches this and other forms of listening)

Listening with the Intent to Empathize or Support

It is my experience that the essential nature of all beings is loving and benevolent. If we happen to be hungry, scared, or pissed off, we might seem a little less loving—but as a whole, being helpful and supportive toward others brings us fulfillment. Unfortunately, without learning effective listening skills, sometimes our best intentions can backfire. For example, if you tell me about a health problem, and my response is to give you the number for my chiropractor, that may not be what you wanted. I may be listening with the *intent* to help, but my response may not *be* helpful, and instead have you feeling missed.

The automatic impulse to help without checking in is sometimes referred to within AR as "caretaking." To truly be helpful, we must train ourselves out of this impulse (which is sometimes an effort to remove our own discomfort, and other times simply a habit). The type of listening that was modeled for many of us was to impulsively do whatever we can to take away someone else's pain.

However, when we share difficult or challenging experiences with another, most often we are looking for empathy—not a quick fix. At the same time, many of us have not yet developed the capacity to explicitly ask for the type listening that we need. So if you are the one listening, keep this in mind. Before offering help, it's usually a safe bet to ask questions that allow the other to express more. There is almost always more underneath the surface, and this kind of presence can build bridges of connection. There may be a time or a place for advice, but instead of assuming, it's always best to check.

At the appropriate moment, you can move into sharing *what it's like* to be with the person you are listening to. In Authentic Relating, we call this "sharing impact."

AR *MASTER* TOOL
Sharing Impact

Sharing impact can be a game-changer because it immediately brings us into the relational level: where your experience and mine meld together, as if we were one living organism.

Here's how it works. Let's say you've just shared something that makes me feel happy. I could say, *Thank you. You are so good to me!* or I could *share impact*: how your words are reverberating in my present moment experience *(e.g.,* "I feel super warm and loved hearing that!"). Sharing our experience with the other is a triple (loving) punch. First, we listen deeply to the movements and currents within ourselves. Second, we practice articulating the nuance of our experience out loud. And last, we share more of ourselves with others, creating connection. That's a lot from one tool!

One note of caution: Be mindful when using this tool to share "negative" impact. It's important to be able to express more challenging feelings like sadness or disappointment, and *Sharing Impact* can be a great way to practice owning our experience. But we shouldn't just share impact and then expect the other person to deal with the emotional burden, and beware to not use this tool in a manipulative way. Setting context around our *intention* (or what we hope for) in sharing challenging experiences is important for creating safety.

Listening with the Intent to Mentor

In Western culture, giving advice tends to be a very common way we respond to others. Sometimes advice is indeed what we're seeking, and can strengthen bonds or relieve a burden. On the other hand, receiving unsolicited advice often feels unpleasant, and sometimes can create disconnection in an instant.

So what's going on here? The key factor is consent. When we feel the impulse to give someone some sage advice or recommend "our lawyer cousin, who handles just those kinds of cases," we must remember to pause first and ask, "Would you like my input, or are you seeking something else?"

Effective use of *listening with the intent to mentor* occurs only when we, 1) have confirmation that our input is wanted, and 2) are approaching the situation with firm belief that the other person already *has* the capacity to handle it. That is, we are not trying to fix anyone, but simply to support. We are the metaphorical hand to help someone get on their feet—rather than taking it upon ourselves to lift them up and carry them.

This sort of listening has a simple, spacious, and honoring quality. To start, try asking, "What would serve you best right now?" and then simply notice how this prompt can often direct someone toward their own inner wisdom.

Listening with the Intent to Appreciate Fully

Each person we encounter has a life as complex and nuanced as our own. It can be a deep stretch for our minds to fully appreciate this, though we all have experiences of seeing someone's depths, or seeing how someone can blossom when we pay them deep attention.

It is ironic that we often miss our own biggest gifts, because they are so ingrained into our essence that we overlook them. We need to be seen by our community and have those gifts appreciated for them to grow. This is where *listening with the intent to appreciate fully* comes in. As Jedi listeners, we can create this type of culture around us by example. When we allow ourselves to experience and acknowledge the qualities that others contribute, we can be the ones to help them see the gifts that are right under their nose.

Akin to the tool from Chapter 6, *Noticing the Gifts of Others,* this mode of listening is an advanced application: It involves deeply listening, witnessing, and experiencing others at the level of the soul. When we look deep enough, we can glimpse another's essence. To listen in this manner, stay present and embodied with the person speaking. When they are finished, you can tell them:

"What I really appreciate about you is..."
"What I really get about you is..."
"The quality I see you bringing to community is..."
or, "You seem uniquely talented at..."

Bids for Connection

According to Gottman, we are constantly making what he calls "bids for connection" toward others.[26] These look like subtle actions or words that implicitly ask for others to

---

26 Gottman, John Mordechai, and Joan DeClaire. *The Relationship Cure: a Five-Step Guide to Strengthening Your Marriage, Family, and Friendships.* Harmony Books, 2002.

give us their attention. A simple example is, "Hey, whatcha doing?" The literal meaning of the question is, "What action are you taking right now?" but the implicit message beneath the words is, "I want connection with you. Are you available?"

When we receive someone's bid for connection, Gottman encourages us to turn toward them. This means that we first have to recognize the implicit request for us to be present and listen. Others are constantly asking for our attention, whether it's stated clearly or not! With this awareness, we can respond to any "bid" with a connected and relational response. In other words, even if we must say no to a specific action, we can still say yes to the connection itself.

According to Gottman, many of the requests we make for connection *are* subtle. It's vulnerable to directly ask for someone's attention, so we often try to *feel* our way into others' availability with subtext. Especially when someone is new to us, it can be easy for us to miss these subtle cues, simply because we all emit and process emotional information differently.

Emotional Availability

This commitment to turn *toward* the people in our lives is the emotional availability that creates lasting and nourishing relationships. It means we won't simply break connection on a whim when we're tired or grumpy. When we are present, embodied, and available to listen to someone, we are investing in the connection. Directly communicating that we are emotionally available to others builds a bridge of trust between us.

Of course, we don't have to be open or available to others all the time, even if we love them. That would be a form of collapse, or honoring others without honoring ourselves. Yet we can still practice opening our heart more often, communicating when it closes, by sharing these afraid or closed down parts of ourselves more vulnerably.

Authenticity is a two-way street. A culture of sharing openly is something that happens naturally between people who are emotionally available and honest. Simply put, we won't share our full selves for very long with someone who is always closing their heart toward us. In this way, the quality of listening that *we* bring to someone can determine the quality of *their* authenticity.

Emotional availability is something that we can feel once we know what to look for. This is the palpable feeling of exchanging emotional energy with each other. In addition to authenticity, emotional availability is the most important quality to bring to our closest relationships. It allows us to feel less alone, more like ourselves, and to have access to interactions that create rich emotional learning.

Chapter 11
EMOTIONAL AIKIDO

You never truly know someone until you fight them.

—Seraphim, *The Matrix*

We can be authentic without blowing up our relationships, *if* we have the proper tools. And through practice, we can learn to transform conflict into clarity, connection, creativity, and teamwork. With the comprehensive set of Authentic Relating tools presented thus far, we can now turn our attention to the ultimate aim of this book: to leverage the energy of conflict, and transform it into honest and creative expression—which, we believe, is the fuel for building thriving communities.

According to Authentic Relating, much of our power rests in the balance point between humility and dignity. To stay in dignity in a difficult situation means that, no matter how the other person is communicating, our own inner voice and compass remains clear and unsuppressed. To reside in humility is to realize that, even if we believe we are right, our view of the situation is partial at best—and furthermore, that every person and situation has something to teach us. On its own, neither capacity is sufficient: We need to develop skills and awareness on both sides.

With great awareness comes great responsibility. One way of gauging our mastery of communication skills is to notice how (if at all) our experience with conflict is changing. As we bring these practices more and more into our lives, we can continuously ask ourselves, "To what degree do my interpersonal challenges dissolve into disconnection, and to what degree do they move toward creativity, collaboration, and mutual growth?"

Remember:

If Conflict = Emotional Energy,
and Dignity + Humility = Transformation,
then Dignity + Humility During Conflict =
Transformation of Emotional Energy

Consider this scene: It's the middle of a large and important business meeting, and tension between two people flares into conflict. The two leaders in the room have already begun raising their voices, and one has challenged the other in front of their employees. The heightened energy in the room has everyone on edge, and neither seems to be backing down. What happens next will affect not only the two involved, but have a ripple effect impacting every person in the room.

Unexpectedly, the leader who was challenged then breaks the tension: "I understand why you're feeling frustrated. I can own that I didn't consider you when I made this decision, and I could have gotten more of your perspective before moving forward." The other leader seems surprised, and after a quiet moment responds, "I appreciate your acknowledging that."

The relief in the room is heard as an audible sigh. Sometimes, a single statement is all that's needed to transform a conflict—steering it toward the harmony that lies at the center of dignity and humility.

What is Conflict and Why is it Valuable?

Conflict can only occur because we care about something. Both sides have something at stake, and are, in some way, attempting to stand for the world that they want to see. Often, the result of this passion is that opposing viewpoints are excluded or demonized. Much can be lost in this stance, but it's worth highlighting that *the passion itself is extremely valuable energy.* In the case of an organization or company, this can be channeled into fueling the mission. AR helps us transform and direct that energy toward what truly matters, and away from attacking others and their values.

A strong community is made up of people who possess such passion: people who are willing to take a stand, and who envision a better future. This is why we speak about *transforming* conflict, instead of *de-escalating* it. We want to harness this energy for our growth—not diminish it!

Having a diversity of values is also crucial for healthy communities. When one person collapses and suppresses their truth, the whole team loses out. The truth is that sometimes we need to fight. Life needs adversity to thrive, and in working through our disagreements, we can discover and express our deepest core values. No muscle can be built without stressing itself repeatedly, and sometimes life requires some wrestling to bring our best ideas into the world.

This concept is exemplified powerfully in an experiment conducted in Arizona in the late 1980s.[27] Researchers were attempting to create an optimal living environment for human, plant, and animal life. They constructed a huge glass dome, which they called "Biosphere 2," to house an artificial, controlled environment with purified air and water, healthy soil, and filtered light. It was assumed that these "ideal" conditions would render optimal growth and thriving for all.

People lived in the biodome for months at a time, and everything seemed to go well—with one exception. The researchers found that when trees grew to a certain height, they would topple over. They were mystified, until they realized they had failed to design in the missing element of *wind*. To grow their strongest, it became clear that trees must experience wind. This is what causes their root systems to grow deeper, supporting the trees as they grow taller.

Let us borrow from this important metaphor. For most of us, the pain of conflict can be such undesirable territory that we avoid it at all costs. Yet without giving ourselves the chance to grow through adversity, we remain underdeveloped. Though our models for conflict may have led us to tense up and resist others and the situation, embracing this metaphorical wind is the only way we can grow stronger.

This is the fundamental shift in awareness that brings about mastery in communication and the ability to transform

---

27   Nelson, Mark. "Pushing Our Limits." 2018, doi:10.2307/j.ctt1zxsmg9.

conflict. It's a 180 degree turn from, "This should not be happening!" to, "This is happening. How can I meet it with dignity and humility?"

Perhaps you are starting to see how the different elements in this book come together to inform our *Emotional Aikido* practice. When we are able to stay somatically grounded in challenging situations, we don't have to resist the defense mechanisms of others—or succumb to our own. Instead, we can actually welcome them. When both sides of a conflict are welcomed and heard, we can channel our differences toward creativity and collaboration. This is the essence of *Emotional Aikido.*

AR POWER TOOL
Relationship Hygiene

We've discussed what can happen when we allow feelings, thoughts, or concerns to be swept under the rug: sickness, depression, anxiety, or disconnection. In short, nothing we'd likely choose consciously!

This tool is a way to prevent such outcomes and, hopefully, even conflict itself before it begins.The shift is to take direct action in your close relationships to discuss challenging topics as they arise—not in an hour, or a day, or a week, but as soon as possible.

This might look like saying:

Can we address what just happened?

Hey, this feels awkward for me, but I want to say it anyway...

I want to talk about something that I imagine may be difficult to hear...

I'm feeling some discomfort around...

While this practice may feel daunting, you can begin the process of developing this skill by committing to talking about small things in your life as they come up. By doing so, we can learn to prevent emotional build-up by voicing our experiences in the moment, as straightforwardly as possible.

This is the essential relationship hygiene that ensures we stay in a place of aliveness and authenticity with those we're closest to. Inauthenticity and resentment are relationship killers, and often when we feel deadness or disconnection with others, it is because we have failed to speak an important truth. This important tool allows us to metaphorically weed the garden, so that we can experience the fruit of connection and nourishment from our relationships.

The Discipline of Aikido

Aikido comes from three words in Japanese. *Ai* means harmony, unity, or "to combine." *Ki* is a term used to describe the spirit of a thing, or the energy. And *do* loosely translates to a path, system, or "way of being." So in English, *Aikido* roughly translates to "the way of unifying energy." Our definition of *Emotional Aikido* is then "the way of transforming emotional energy into harmony."

The discipline of Aikido is an apt metaphor to represent a convergence of many AR skills, because of its philosophy of unity. An authentic conversation is one in which both people leave changed, because there is listening and sharing happening in both directions. The poet David Whyte beautifully illustrates this in his statement, *There is no fixed sense of self that will survive a real conversation.*[28] The aim of the *Emotional Aikido* process is to foster the emotional intelligence that allows us to have this type of true conversation.

Once we can appreciate that a triggered person's nervous system is effectively shutting them down in order to protect them, and we can respond with compassion (even in the face

---

28   Whyte, David. "Courageous Conversations."." Kripalu. Feb. 2015. Lecture. https://youtu.be/fl58ny_6AFc.

of blame), then we will have reached a real milestone in our development. This is when we'll have developed the ability to *respond instead of react*. When successful, this process helps both people move out of patterns of posture and collapse, and into patterns of dignity and humility. And with enough practice, it becomes possible to lead the way for others into this more grounded space.

The harmony I am speaking of here is not some hippie cliché. It is a fierce and generous love that takes courage and fortitude to hold. This type of love is so expansive that it can hold all our differing perspectives, and cradle both parties' emotions with care. This flavor of love is large enough to hold our differences and even strife.

The Five Steps of Emotional Aikido

Emotional Aikido is a five-step process for skillfully transmuting charge that is directed at you. The next chapter, *Emotional Alchemy,* describes how to be and what to do when you are the one who is charged. "Charge," in this context, could mean anger, upset, anxiety, fear or grief. Together, these two practices form the culmination of our Authentic Relating toolkit.

It's important to note that the Five Practices from Chapter 3 are foundational to both *Emotional Aikido* and *Emotional Alchemy.* If we are attempting to welcome everything and assume nothing, and if we are practicing revealing and owning our experience in a way that honors self and other, then the following skills will be much more natural and effective to employ.

Before going into more depth, let's start with a short summary.

Step 1: Do Nothing

Breathe. Ground yourself. Connect to your body. In simple terms, "Do Nothing" means getting present with ourselves, instead of reacting to whatever the other is bringing.

Step 2: Completely Listen

Create a space of listening for the other person, by letting them know that you want to hear them fully. Ask clarifying questions to signal that you sincerely want to understand. However they're behaving, underneath is a person with needs, who is simply trying to get those needs met.

Step 3: Reflect and Validate

As best you can, reflect back what the person is saying in your own words. Remember that the other person's perspective is true and valid in their experience—whether or not you understand or agree. What they feel matters to them. Let them know it matters to you too.

Step 4: Ownership

Take responsibility for your impact on the situation. Acknowledge your choices and any mistakes you might have made. If appropriate, apologize with dignity—but don't collapse into an apology as an automatic appeasement.

Step 5: Share Impact

Start including your perspective by sharing your in-the-moment impact. How does it *feel* to receive this information? What you feel matters more than your viewpoint, and your thoughts or judgments about the information should follow only when there's a clear signal to do so. Remember: Connection first. Correction last.

Note: *Emotional Aikido* is a tool for situations that you either *want to* or *must* be in. Remember that sometimes (e.g., in cases of physical or emotional abuse), removing ourselves from engagement with a person completely is the appropriate and necessary response.

Now, let's consider each of these steps of *Emotional Aikido* more deeply.

Step 1: Do Nothing

Often when we disagree with someone, our brain's automatic defenses kick in. To the extent that the topic of disagreement is important to us, our instinct is to react quickly to protect our values and beliefs. To mitigate the obvious problems inherent in such automatic responses, it is our job to practice *slowing down.* Rather than react and *do,* this step asks us to simply *be.* By remaining in a stance of nonreaction (even for a short period) when someone is angry or upset, we set ourselves up for a much more fruitful interaction.

Practically, this looks like: taking a deep breath, feeling your feet on the ground, bringing your awareness into your body, and perhaps even inviting the other person to do the same with you. If the other person is calm enough to do so, this last request can be a great strategy for slowing the conversation down in the heat of the moment.

If we react by throwing our emotional defenses up, or immediately sharing our own perspective, we can easily find ourselves locked in a battle of wills. Through practicing *Emotional Aikido*, we can instead stay connected and centered within ourselves throughout. Remember: Your soft, slow breath keeps you connected to your body—your most valuable source of information during conflict.

When we develop this skill, we will have achieved the first level of mastery within AR: *the ability to respond instead of react.* This is a great phrase to carry into our lives in all situations, as a concise way to remember the practice of *Emotional Aikido.*

Step 2: Completely Listen

In this calm and centered place, more emotional energy and empathy becomes available. We can set aside the need to defend ourselves immediately, and instead simply listen. Sometimes just letting someone know you want to hear them is in itself the antidote to conflict. Where the other may have expected our own reactive posturing, by hearing out intent to listen, they may now feel resourced enough to move toward a more collaborative orientation.

Of course, this doesn't mean that your inner seven-year-old won't be complaining, and conjuring up reasons that they're wrong and you're right. We all have an inner child that believes we are being singled out or unfairly accused. While we can recognize this voice as valid and trust in its good intentions, we must also be willing to set it aside for the sake of this practice. Remember that there will be a time and place for sharing your own perspective—and it's not during this step.

To complete this step, check in with the other:

"Is there more you want to share?" or,
"Are you feeling complete?"

Step 3: Reflect and Validate

What you feel matters—no matter what it is. Our emotions are real, energetic experiences, and far too often are invalidated or dismissed by others. Too much of this invalidation, and we can become understandably sensitive around our need to be heard. Whether we are met in this need makes the difference between our nervous system being in a state of safety and calm, or hyper-aroused and under threat.

To reflect and validate the other's words, try starting with one of the following:

"Can I tell you what I'm hearing?"
"What I think you're saying is…"
"I want to make sure I understand you…"

This simple act of reflection can do both parties a great service. When someone feels heard and understood, they become better able to self-regulate—which may contribute to greater receptivity to hearing *your* perspective later on (but not yet!).

Do your best not to take what they are sharing personally, and when in doubt, remember the importance of both humility and dignity. The mantra, "I have something to learn from this situation," can be helpful when you find yourself moving toward posturing. And if you find yourself falling into harsh self-judgment or collapse, remember that their perspective, too, is partial at best.

Note that all the reflection in the world can't guarantee the other person won't continue to fuel the conflict. We can only control ourselves, and our own choice to embody *Emotional Aikido*. We can choose to remain peaceful and open, trusting that our own perspective is valid, whether or not the other is capable of hearing it. We can remind ourselves of all we don't know, and that we need others to see our own blind spots. This practice is not easy, but tremendously kind—to both ourselves and the other.

After reflecting, try asking this follow-up question:

"I want to make sure I am understanding you. Can you correct me in anything I may have misunderstood?"

With this follow-up, we are signaling to the other person that their perspective is important, and that we are willing to be wrong. We can then close by asking: "Did I miss anything?"

Step 4: Ownership

When we "own" (or take responsibility for) something we have said or done, we let the other person know that they are safe and that they matter. When threatened, some of us become demanding and urgent (posturing), while some of us have learned to make ourselves small and appease the other (collapsing). In either case, our willingness to take ownership can eliminate the sense of threat, creating a more conducive atmosphere for constructive conversation.

These look like simple statements that acknowledge our contribution to the conflict we are in (e.g., "I own that I could have been more thoughtful in ensuring you were copied on the email chain"). We can also make small follow-up commitments that seek to address whatever hurt has occurred (e.g., "In the future, I will do my best to make sure you're kept informed").

Of course, none of these steps will be effective if we're not genuine. Be mindful that, in anything you own, it's an action you can truly take responsibility for. Remember: Ownership is a presence, not just the words we use—and our sincerity (or lack thereof) comes through in every aspect of our being.

Note: You might need to make multiple statements (or even go back to Step 1 and 2) before the other person can truly relax. Remember that transforming conflict takes time, commitment, and care—so do your best to be patient, and trust that each step is ultimately moving the conversation forward.

Step 5: Sharing Impact

So far, we have been considering *Emotional Aikido* in the context of conflict, but these steps can be just as applicable in any "charged" situation. If in conflict, this specific sequencing is recommended. If not, you can always try practicing each step independently.

Whatever the situation, this last step is key for creating connection and presence (and should always come before sharing your perspective, if in conflict). When we share *perspective*, we share thoughts, opinions and judgments around the past. When we share *impact*, we share feelings and observations about the present moment. As we explored in Chapter 10, this is a master tool, central to AR, in which we let the other person know what is happening for us in relation to them right now. We include the fullness of our human experience, and model that it is safe for both of us to express our emotions and challenges. Their response, in this case, is also a source of feedback, indicating if they are ready for a calm and present exchange.

After you share impact, if their response is still charged, it may mean that one or more of the previous steps needs revisiting in order for them to feel safe and heard. It also may be that the exchange needs a pause, before engaging in the steps again as needed. Being able to handle the discomfort of a pause in unresolved conflict is also an *Emotional Aikido* skill.

If all goes smoothly, we can then get consent to share our perspective:

"Is it okay if I share my thoughts on this with you?"

After following these steps more deliberately, the conversation may become more free-flowing and organic. Think of each step as a brick that we lay to create a foundation of trust. From this basis, communicating authentically becomes far safer, and we need not feel so threatened by the other person's truth.

AR POWER TOOL
Speaking the Moment

It's the beginning of a workshop, and everyone is going around the circle checking in. Most shares are brief and simple—being curious how the day will go, or tired and needing their morning coffee. The next person to share looks clearly distraught and announces, "One of my close friends passed away yesterday, and I'm not sure if I can make it through the workshop today." The room goes quiet, and no one seems to know how to respond.

We've all been in situations where we feel the energy of a group freeze. Maybe everyone was aware of a certain "elephant in the room," but no one wanted to be the one to acknowledge it. When this happens, it often feels like we are simply waiting for an uncomfortable moment to end—or for someone else to rescue us from it. This is a particular type of inauthenticity that happens when we feel psychologically unsafe or uncomfortable, and don't want to take the risk of fully expressing ourselves. Perhaps we feel shy or worry about being judged, or even think we are being nice by ignoring the interaction. This is a tool to address all of these situations skillfully.

The next time you find yourself in an "awkward" group dynamic, see what happens when instead, you *Speak the Moment*. This means that we name, rather than avoid, what we are witnessing occuring. In the example above, that might look like: *It seems like none of us know how to respond. I wonder if there is a way the group could support you right now?*

Simple acknowledgments like this are a service to the group as a whole—such tension and awkwardness can rarely survive being named. By *Speaking the Moment*, we are keeping the energy flowing rather than stuck.

This tool doesn't just apply to uncomfortable situations; simply naming what is happening can be useful in many contexts. For example: *We seem to be tired and finished with this game. We don't seem to be giving George space to speak his mind. Does anyone else feel like we are missing something?* In each instance, we not only allow for self-expression, but also give voice to the previously unnamed. This is a stance of true leadership.

The Way of The Open Heart

As we begin more fully embodying the tools of AR, we become more courageous to name the previously unnameable. Even though, on the whole, this is a pathway to greater harmony, in the moment it can often feel like going through "growing pains." In other words, paradoxically, we may find ourselves moving through more conflict than we were before.

It's important to keep in mind that it is not our responsibility to "fix" all of the conflict that shows up in our lives. But it *is* our responsibility to do our best with the people that matter to us: to show up in these connections with honesty, empathy, and grace.

As with traditional Aikido, the practice of *Emotional Aikido* is all about staying centered and grounded. This is not about leveraging the other's energy against them, but using that energy to create deeper connection. Connection can feel pleasant and nourishing, but it can also feel painful or uncomfortable. The truth is that "connection" simply means facing the truth, together—which sometimes can even mean a conscious separation. Yet even if the relationship must end, through practicing *Emotional Aikido*, we can navigate the separation with more harmony and awareness.

Keep in mind, dignity is never urgent or overbearing. We simply have our truth, and we can wait until the other is receptive enough to hear it. And it's true that sometimes, a person may never be ready. In these times, we can return to the wisdom of *Welcome Everything*—even if that means a conflict going unresolved.

Chapter 12
EMOTIONAL ALCHEMY

You can't always get what you want, but if you try sometimes, you just might find, you get what you need.

—THE ROLLING STONES

If left unchecked, our survival instincts are strong enough to run amok and destroy our society. This is why humans have developed laws, regulations, police forces, and armies—yet these powerful instincts are a permanent part of us. They are not going anywhere, and suppressing them never works for long. In Authentic Relating, we allow the full power of these instincts to be expressed, without letting them take over and wreak havoc in our relationships.

Balancing these mighty forces can create a tremendous source of vitality in our life. This skill is far from easy, and yet necessary to develop in our journey into maturity.

We all have experienced moments when we chose not to speak up, even when our intuition whispered, "This isn't right." We simply were not clear or courageous enough to speak the truth. This doesn't make us inauthentic—it makes us human. *Emotional Alchemy* is the opposite of the suppression or repression of our experience. With training, we can instead dig into our truth in those moments, and bring that truth to light with the people we care about. We can choose to express instead of suppress. This opens a process of vital digestion and metabolization of our experience, and the result is more available emotional energy.

Alchemy Principles

Alchemy is the ancient study of turning lead into gold. In *Emotional Alchemy*, we are doing the difficult yet sacred work of transforming a "withhold" into an opportunity. Withholds are all the things we don't share with others—out of fear, resistance, judgment, or avoidance of potential emotional backlash—but that could have some value if we had the courage to express them. When we withhold, we are effectively repressing our true selves, in a misguided attempt to maintain ease in a relationship.

Unfortunately, this rarely works. Repression leads to a buildup of dissonance and tension, which, over time, only damage our bodies and minds. With the five steps of *Emotional Alchemy*, we return that energy to a more harmonious state by releasing the withheld communication. It's the final tool we will cover, because it is a culmination of everything we have learned throughout this journey.

Think of a time you experienced the relief of telling the truth. Telling the truth just feels good—and that feeling of relief is the transformation of stagnant into useful and *usable* energy. Learning to do this in real-time is one of the most powerful skills you can master. Just as alchemists transform metal into gold, we can learn to transform conflict into love. When we willingly embrace every energy, emotion, and experience as the precious material that it is, there's no limit to the depths of connection we can create.

AR POWER TOOL
Slow Down to Feel More

This tool is simply a mantra: *Slow down to feel more.*

It works for every sensation, from feeling the air on our skin and hearing the birds outside, to sensing our feelings of right and wrong. The more slowly and softly we approach an experience, the more sensitive we can be to the information contained therein.

This tool points us to a profound reality: Our sensitivity and our intelligence are connected. Our ability to learn is directly related to our capacity for openness and subtlety. This openness can be directed within, to notice and interpret information from our bodies or intuition. Or, it can be directed externally, to notice and interpret information from others and life itself.

When we are in a conversation with someone important in our lives, we can simply repeat to ourselves, *Slow down to feel more.* In this way, we can keep pace with our organic nature while in connection with others.

This is also an incredible tool for cultivating pleasure in our lives. Slowing down to feel more can open up delicious avenues for appreciating anything from food to sex, to any number of delightful experiences. The cherry on top? All of this will help reduce our tolerance for incongruence in relationships, and fuel our resolve to practice Authentic Relating.

Congruence and Coherence

Before we look at the steps of *Emotional Alchemy,* we must understand something important about the issue of trust in human relationships. When we don't trust someone, there are generally two reasons: we are reacting to our past conditioning, or we are perceiving a very real incongruence in the other. Confusingly, it's often a mix of the two. This is why we need to learn to explore our differences through conversation; there is almost always a wealth of valuable learning for all parties involved.

(Note: What I've just written assumes an absence of the possibility of real physical harm. Mistrust evolved for a reason, so I am not talking here about situations where danger is relevant, and where self-protective measures are absolutely called for.)

Because just about everyone in the world has had their trust shattered at some point, most humans are highly sensitive to dishonesty and duplicity. After all, our very survival depends on this ability. With a finely-tuned nervous system, sometimes we can literally *feel* inauthentic behaviors. If you've ever heard or said something like, "That person makes my skin crawl," this may be an example of this sensitivity in action. We can sense ulterior motives, or that something is being hidden from us. Within AR this is known as *noticing dissonance.*

Of course, we are not always right. Our senses are sending us messages, but assuming those messages are accurate quickly gets us into trouble. Fear is a primary survival mechanism. When we believe we sense inauthenticity in others, we tend immediately to categorize the person as bad, wrong, or untrustworthy. However, the "pattern-recognition software" in our brains often extrapolates or projects. It is designed to protect us, after all, and can take mistrust too far, too fast.

Instead, if we take a moment to zoom out, we might remember that every one of us has moments of incongruence and internal dissonance, and that others have likely felt this way about us! This can restore a tiny bit of faith in the other person. Once that is extended, we can then engage in a conversation to clear the "withhold," instead of throwing them under the proverbial bus. This can be seen as a type of relationship hygiene: We clear out any of the dust or murkiness in our connection, until it feels fresh and good to be around one another.

So, the next time your alarm bells go off about someone's behavior, you can choose to pause and consider whether you really have all the facts. Bringing the dissonance that you feel to this person in a skill way can result in connection, clarity, and be a great gift for them. Remember, the practice of *Assume Nothing* is foundational, and a form of kindness we can bring to others.

Learning to tune into the feeling of congruence (in ourselves and others) is an important capacity to cultivate for *Emotional Alchemy*. After all, in conflict (of which mistrust is an early indicator), we are playing with volatile emotional "chemicals," and attempting to transmute them. If you know anything about alchemy, you'll appreciate that it's a heated process!

AR *MASTER* TOOL
Make Clear and Vulnerable Requests

Often the word "vulnerability" is associated with being exposed in our weaknesses, insecurities or challenges. But remember, *courage* is an everyday vulnerability. Speaking the truth, even when our voice shakes, is the primary way we can build our muscles of courage.

A clear and concise way to practice this with the people in our lives is to make clear and vulnerable requests regarding our needs and wants. In a sense, this is a shortcut to transmuting our complaints into constructive communication. When we cease to judge and blame, and instead own our experience, we can begin to process items that come up in our awareness very quickly.

It goes a little something like this. A difficult experience arises and you identify that something feels emotionally off. You give yourself a few minutes to stop judging the heck out of the other person and find a sense of ownership. Usually, this will culminate in a realization of your next clear action. *(I need to initiate a conversation with this person about _____. To approach it skillfully, I will make a clear and vulnerable request.)*

At this point, the alchemy within you has already begun. Much of your emotional energy can release, and you'll probably feel relief *even before you have the conversation.*

The next step is actually making that *clear and vulnerable request*. This might look like:

Hey honey, when you want to discuss weekend plans and I'm in the middle of something, I feel stressed. I want to give both things my attention, but I can't do both at once. Would it be alright if we set aside time for those types of talks?

In this way, we move through experiences of potential conflict with more ease, agency and flow. By being clear, direct, and vulnerable, we are serving those around us, as well as our own creative and relational energy.

The Five Steps of Emotional Alchemy

These five steps are here for you to call upon whenever you are upset, angry, or emotionally activated—whether that's before or during a conversation. As we did in the last chapter, we'll consider each of the steps briefly so you can see an overview of the process. Then, we'll explore each one in more depth.

Note: This process can be done externally (in conversation), or internally (through journaling or active contemplation). I advise you to start small when using these practices, before moving on to address issues that involve more deeply-ingrained patterns.

Step 1: Connection Over Content

Ask yourself: Who is this person to you? (A new friend? Valued business partner? A lover or spouse you hope to spend the rest of your life with?) Keep that in mind, and then let them know by stating this expressly as you start the conversation. Commit to the connection itself as a valuable part of this exchange.

Step 2: Context

Share your *why* and *want* for the conversation, before you share your *what* (which you won't share until after Step 3).

Step 3: Consent

Enlist consent. Attempting to push past someone's defenses almost never works. Asking permission to express anger, upset, or give someone feedback helps ensure they'll be receptive to your communication.

Step 4: Communicate

First share the objective facts, to create shared reality. Then share your interpretations and your feelings (the *what*), in a way that is owned.

Step 5: Check for Impact

After you have shared, check for the impact of your statements. Ask, "How does this affect you in this moment, or our relationship as a whole?" Be open to hearing another perspective, even (and especially!) if it differs from yours.

Step 1: Connection Over Content

There is a good reason why humans often shy away from conflict. If we go into it with guns blazing, without tools and skills to handle it, relationships can fall apart and people can get fired. In other words, there is the potential for social destructiveness, and even our most important relationships are not immune.

This principle of *Connection Over Content* means ensuring that we are in touch with the value of the relationship, *before* we attempt to communicate what we are challenged by. J. Krishnamurti may have said this best:

> *Action has meaning only in relationship, and without understanding relationship, action on any level will only breed conflict. The understanding of relationship is infinitely more important than the search for any plan of action.*[29]

These words suggest that our relationship should be held as the first priority—and that if we are not in touch with the deep value it holds, we will inevitably make a mess of the entire situation. We do this by first noticing and expressing *who* the person is to us, and what our relationship with them means. If you have been practicing the *Psychological Safety Net* tool from Chapter 7, you may have already started tuning in to your deeper appreciations for people, and saying those things out loud to them.

This can be accomplished in a variety of ways. In essence, we express: There is a connection here, and that connection is about...

---

29   Krishnamurti, J. "Action and Relationship." *Colombo Ceylon.* Jan. 1950. Lecture.

Step 2: Context

Setting an effective context is essential to alchemizing any conflict—so much so that we gave "context" an entire chapter! For our *Emotional Alchemy* practice, we set context to enroll others in conversations that may be challenging or scary. We share our sincerest hopes for the outcome, as a way of creating buy-in. We can also share any fears we may have, as a way of expressing our own vulnerability. Here's a couple examples of what this might look like:

> "Mike, I want to initiate a conversation around some things that have been challenging in our work together, and I'm confident we can work through our different perspectives in this. My hope is that we'll both come out of this talk with more understanding, and do better work as a result."

> "Sarah, I want to address that fight we had a month ago. I'm a bit scared that you'll feel annoyed, because you might already be over it. But I think if I can express some things that still feel leftover for me, I'll feel more comfortable and trusting around you going forward."

It's important to emphasize: *The context is not the content.* Our intention here is to prepare the other person to receive our communication, but an essential step remains. We can offer a quick "headline" for the content (think of a newspaper heading or Tweet), but before diving in any further, we must get their consent.

Step 3: Consent

The word "consent" comes from the Latin "consentire": *con* meaning "together", and *sentire* meaning "to feel." In this way, consent is a type of emotional resonance. The musical term of "consonance" (the opposite of dissonance) has a similar meaning, describing two notes that sound harmonious in unison. We can look at consent between people in much the same way—and as a means by which emotional information can freely flow.

This ability to "feel together" can be deliberately developed and practiced. Questions like, "Is that okay with you?" or "Is now a good time?" are all ways to foster consent. It's also important, after we ask, to be aware of both the verbal *and* nonverbal response we receive.

Remember, in this place of resonance, we can digest and process infinitely more emotional energy (*1 + 1 = 11!*). But if we try to speak our truth by pushing beyond someone's boundaries, *Emotional Alchemy* will be impossible. This is why consent is central to our ability to transform energy.

Step 4: Communicate

With connection, context, and consent clearly established, the content of our difficult conversations has much more space to breathe. We can now communicate the *what*: our thoughts, emotions and observations about the conflict. It is highly recommended that you start with something "objective," or to begin by communicating about things that are observably true. This can allow for a sense of shared understanding, before moving into the murkier territory of feelings.

For example, "Remember when we were having a discussion about your sister yesterday?"

Remember, this step is a continuation of the "alchemy," not our chance to finally vent. In other words, we must own the experience we want to share. As discussed in Chapter 3, ownership is an understanding that we (like everyone else) are responsible for our own experiences. Our friend didn't "make" us angry—though we may have felt anger after something she did. Our emotions are true and valid for us, but they are never the whole story.

A helpful tool is to speak in statements that are precise and undebatable. While someone could argue with, "You left me stranded," the phrase, "When you decided to quit, I felt disappointed and hurt," leaves little room for debate. Similarly, "I notice this has happened twice before in the past," is more owned (and more accurate) than, "You always do this." In all of these examples, we are moving from making claims about reality to owning our subjective experience.

Brené Brown, a pioneer in the field of vulnerability research, suggests using the statement, "The story I'm making up is…"[30] This can be a brilliant way of owning what is happening for us without blaming or putting it on the other person.

After sharing, it's important to leave room for feedback—and in fact, to explicitly invite it. A simple, "I want to make sure that made sense to you, and hear your thoughts on what I've said," can be a powerful indicator of psychological safety. It signals that we are flexible, and willing to be corrected.

---

30   Brown, Brené. *Rising Strong: How the Ability to Reset Transforms the Way We Live, Love, Parent, and Lead.* Random House, 2017.

Rather than stirring their defensiveness, we invite new perspectives and clarity. This *openness to being changed* is at the heart of *Emotional Alchemy*. Where ownership is our dignity, this vulnerability is our humility. After all, being stubborn and being transformed don't really mix.

This approach then becomes an invitation for others to reciprocate, and arriving at such mutual understanding is often a visceral, embodied experience. Palpable sensations of relaxation or new energy can be great indicators of our success in the practice of alchemy.

Step 5: Check for Impact

This step takes us back to the concept of polarity. Authenticity, or truth-telling, is always followed by receptivity. We don't drop "truth bombs" and walk away, or only honor ourselves while forgetting the other. Just like the cycle of precipitation, we pour (or express) and then absorb (or listen)—and keep repeating this process, over and over again.

To check for impact, we can ask, "How is that for you to hear?" or "What happens for you when I share this?" We simply pass the proverbial talking stick back, while establishing ourselves in humility. We stay open to what we might learn in the conversation.

In this stance of dignity and humility, we can create a *shared reality*: the emotional territory upon which we build our relationships. Knowing the felt sense of shared reality is important in leading us toward states of congruence within ourselves and our relationships. Remember the words of George Bernard Shaw: *The single biggest problem in communication is the illusion that it has taken place.* If we do not check for impact, we run the risk of further misunderstandings. But when we both "know that we know," the feeling is palpable—and wonderfully connective.

CONCLUSION

Weaving shared reality is an exchange of communication where you both come to understand that there are some things that are true for you and true for them, and you both know that's the case. Our ability to further explore, create, and discover shared reality together is a fundamental and ever-present human possibility, and a marvel of existence.

—MICHAEL PORCELLI (AR LEADER)

When I was 10 years old, there were about 12 television stations: three mainstream networks (ABC, NBC, and CBS), plus the public station PBS, and a handful of other local and regional ones. You could also pay a little extra for HBO and a few other premium stations. By the time I left my parents' house for college, there were literally hundreds of available channels. A few years after that, cable TV included nearly a thousand channels. Today, there are millions of websites that provide entertainment and news of all types.

We are living an experience of diversity and complexity that far exceeds anything our parents or grandparents experienced. In this climate, it is virtually impossible to know what is objective truth. While we might accept this concept theoretically, let's pause just for a moment to consider the very real societal consequences. Political discord in the United States alone negatively impacts millions, when we consider the detrimental policies advanced (or beneficial policies held back) due to poor conflict-resolution and connection-building skills.

All of this highlights the reason that I believe Authentic Relating is such an important practice for humanity at this time. We are living an experience of diversity and complexity that far exceeds anything our parents or grandparents experienced. Because of these trends, creating "shared reality" is a critical skill that will only increase in importance. The world's ever-expanding nature means that we will need to grapple with this complexity in our hearts and minds, together with our communities. If we're to survive and thrive as a species, we must become larger in our hearts and minds, and bring care and compassion to people who think, look, and behave differently than we do.

The Purpose of Conflict

I invite you to try on this belief of mine and see if it fits for you: If we do not learn the lessons of the conflicts, tensions, and difficulties in our lives right now, they will only keep returning. Or, as one of my teachers put it, "If we fail the test, we just get to take it again, and again, and again until we pass. Isn't that kind?"

We already know that conflict can create energy—but I also believe it is much bigger than that. Conflict is a dense energy packet from the universe that can be difficult to decipher (and even harder to transmute), but it points the way to exactly the lessons we need to learn in order to grow. In other words, I believe conflict is the universe helping us to become more self-defined, and to set appropriate boundaries so that our energy can be used constructively.

Humanizing Technology

Recently I was at a park, and saw a father changing his child's diaper. Even though the child was not even two, she was intently watching the father's iPhone, her little hands clinging to the device as naturally as anything. She was mesmerized by the dancing screen.

Children become glued to their devices at ever-younger ages. Those screens now go with them everywhere. And as adults, we can be even worse! The car, bedroom, and even outdoors—all these are places we "plug in" and "tune out." We frequently focus our attention on a few square inches of small electronic display—yet embodiment is in 360 degrees, using all five senses. As a society, we are only a decade or so into an experiment on the potentially drastic effects of mobile devices on both our brains and our relationships.

I'm not saying that this technology is inherently bad. I *am* saying it has become extremely pervasive within a short period of time, and may have negative effects on social health if we don't develop our relational skills. We don't yet know the combined effects of such an influential and even addictive element in our lives.

As we navigate this mass stimulation and rapid societal adoption of tech, I believe the most important thing to keep in mind is that *being* connected and *feeling* connected are two different things. We can be surrounded by people, but when we are relating from our pasts or our projected personas, we will probably still feel lonely and disconnected. Social media can often reinforce these masks, presenting "touched up" and synthesized versions of our lives. The questions then arise: What is authenticity in the digital age? What is the "true" self?

A good place to start is by simply noticing our tendency to cover up our insecurities. From here, we can choose to get more real and more "revealed"—both on and offline.

Authentic Relating as a Balance Point

From the moment we are born, our development is shaped by the grace of another human being's desire to fulfill our inherent needs. This giving and receiving is a tangible, practical form of love. As we grow older, our identity continues to be shaped by the way we are seen, heard, and received by others. I don't believe we find our true and authentic self in isolation, but rather that our identities are formed and uncovered through every relationship we have.

And relationships are a changing thing in today's world of social media. It is my belief that in this divided climate, our emotional energy is our most precious commodity. Authentic Relating is a balancing force to the tremendous influence that technology will continue to have on our culture, and might even be described as a powerful counterbalancing *social technology.* Not only can it teach us to feel and speak our needs and desires, it can allow us to band together to create a greater good. We can choose to communicate with others from a place of more self-understanding, getting our needs for love and belonging met while also learning how to love others better.

Is it possible to intentionally develop ourselves in the art of giving and receiving love? I believe so, and it's why I created this book. I've seen it time and time again in my Authentic Relating facilitating and consulting. And in a complex technological world, these skills need to be taught for the well-being of all.

With these practices now in your hands, your heart, and your mind, you can bring this art of giving and receiving love to the world. Thank you for being part of this growing Authentic Relating movement. We need your soft heart and sharp mind.

ADDITIONAL AR GAMES

CORE GAMES

There are literally hundreds of Authentic Relating Games you can play, offering a wide variety of experiences. AR Games can involve fun and silliness, movement, soul-searching, and even helps us practice setting boundaries. They can blend with improv theater, provide rest and nourishment, and help us learn more about each other. They grow our emotional awareness in a myriad of ways.

Of these hundreds, there are nine Core Games that are most foundational to AR's Five Practices, and which form the basic underpinnings of many additional games. Three of these core games were discussed in Part II: The Noticing Game, The Gratitude Game, and Curiosity. Here, we will dive into the remaining six.

Note: There is an additional resource available from Authentic Revolution (www.authrev.org) that lists and details an extensive number of AR games (over 150 of them). In this book, we will focus on the essence and purpose of a handful of core games, plus a few "bonus" games that are more light-hearted and fun. All of these can be adapted and modified to suit various environments, audiences, and moods.

Empathy

Length: 25–30 minutes

Configuration: Pairs

Related Teachings: Reveal Your Experience; Honor Self and Other; Listening

The Empathy Game (or simply "Empathy") is directly designed to help us practice the modes of listening discussed in Chapter 9. This game is arguably the most potent for working directly with our "heart muscle"—our critical human capacity to deeply feel and "see" others. It also helps us break the habit of "listening to reply," and train our ability to ask for what we really need.

There are four rounds to this game, each of which exercises a different facet of empathy:

- Reflective listening
- Sharing impact
- Optional advice (with consent)
- Noticing others' gifts

Instructions for Playing:

Choose a Person A and a Person B. Person A will share first, and Person B will listen. (At the end, we'll switch roles and repeat.)

- Choose a prompt, which Person A will speak on. This prompt can be broad or specific, but is intended to hone in on something that is meaningful for the sharer (e.g *What's on your heart right now?* or *What is something important happening in your life at this time?*).

- **Round 1:** A shares. (3 minutes)
- **Round 2:** To the best of their ability, B reflects back exactly what they heard A share, without adding any of their own opinions, perspective, or impact. (1 minute)
- **Round 3:** A clarifies any important pieces that were misunderstood, or goes deeper with their sharing. (3 minutes)
- **Round 4:** B shares the impact, using ownership language.
  - *e.g., When you shared ___, I felt ___, or, The place I felt you the most was... (1 minute)*
- **Round 5:** B asks: *What's an obstacle related to this important thing?* and A shares their answer. (2 minutes)
- **Round 6:** B asks: *Do you want advice?* or the softer: *Do you want to hear my thoughts on this?*
- If A says yes, B may give advice, if it feels authentic for them. If A doesn't want advice, they can request something they do want (e.g., *Would you give me a hug? Could I actually just vent a bit more?* or *Let's just be in silence*). (1 minute)
- **Round 7:** B shares their new understanding with A, including an appreciation about them as a person. (1 minute)
  - *e.g., What I really get about you is... or The Values I see you standing for are..*

Anything Goes

Length: 10–15 minutes
Configuration: Pairs
Related Teachings: Welcome Everything, Reveal Your Experience

The game is all about expression and embodiment, and can be a powerful window into unconscious thoughts and feelings. In Anything Goes, self-inquiry is a "full human" practice. We inquire into our experience through several different channels, switching between them to explore multiple possibilities. We also practice *Welcoming Everything*: moving our experience through literally moving our bodies, in ways that connect us more deeply with the full range of our emotional, mental, physical, or even spiritual landscape.

Most importantly, we do this while being witnessed by another person. While we may not be sharing anything explicitly in words, what is revealed can be profound. In the presence of a silent supportive party, we have more capacity for digesting and metabolizing our experience—and we practice inhabiting the perhaps uncomfortable space of being "seen."

Instructions for Playing:

Have participants choose who will start as the "expresser" and who will start as the "witness." The witness should be seated about 4–6 feet away. Typically, the expresser begins in a standing position, though beginning on hands and knees or lying on one's back are also options.

For 3–5 minutes, "Anything Goes" for the expresser. That could look like verbal sharing, yelling, silence, moving, growling, singing, dancing, or anything in between—with as much or as little eye contact with their witness as they desire. Witnesses should remain silent throughout, with a simple, supportive presence.

After the timer goes off, be sure to remind everyone to transition slowly, allowing at least a minute for the expresser to come out. In this game, we can go deep—touching parts of ourselves that are unfamiliar or even frightening. To safely ground the expresser back into the here and now, the witness should ask what is called an "attention out" question: something that prompts the person to re-engage with their physical and social surroundings (e.g., *What color is the wall?* or *What did you have for breakfast?* or *Where did you get those jeans you're wearing?*). Once the expresser confirms they're feeling grounded and ready to continue, switch roles and repeat.

Game Game

Length: 30–40 minutes
Configuration: Groups of 3–4
Related Teachings: Context-Setting, Culture Creation;
Honor Self and Other

If you watch children play, they are creating games all the time. "You be the tiger, and I will be the unicorn!" In essence, these are no different from the "games" we create as adults—though as adults, we usually don't have as much fun! One of the themes of Authentic Relating is being intentional about the games we play, or in other words, setting context effectively.

Game Game helps us reconcile these two worlds, harnessing our childlike imagination so we can set contexts we want to be part of. In other words, it's about envisioning an experience we want to create (Context-Setting), and then communicating that context in a way that enrolls others (Culture Creation). While many AR Games develop these skills indirectly, Game Game may be the simplest as well as the most versatile in its application.

In this game, each participant gets 10 minutes to create anything their heart desires—from role-playing Harry Potter to making a plot for world peace. As we explored earlier, the way we communicate our vision is just as important as the vision itself. The more we can convey our deep "why" to others, the more enthusiastic they're likely to be about playing. In this way, Game Game can be a source of great insight into our leadership. Do people resist our vision? Do they seem naturally excited? We can consider this helpful feedback, either way!

As the facilitator, you will need to teach a little bit about setting context. Though we explored some more abstract facets of context in Chapter 9, this skill, Game Game brings us back to its simplest definition: the *who, what, how, where, and why.*

Instructions for Playing:

As the Player: Set Context:
- **Who?** Who's going to play?
- **What?** What's involved? Do we need any materials or tools?
- **How?** How is the game played? What are the rules? Are there any qualities that we want to embody?
- **Where?** What's the physical space? Any limits?
- **Why?** Why do you want to play? What's your underlying need or desire (e.g., expression, creativity, rest, or connection)?
  - *This is what I find really appealing about this context/ game...*
  - *This is why I've found it to really work in the past...*
  - *This is why I imagine you'd really enjoy the game/get value out of it...*
- Have everyone get into groups, and pick someone to go first. This person tunes into what they're really wanting right now, and then creates a game or experience that aligns with this desire (or chooses a game they're already familiar with).

- They then have two minutes to set context for the group, answering any clarifying questions, and incorporating any feedback until the others feel enrolled.
- Then for 8 minutes—play! (Note: The context-setter is the context-holder. They're responsible for observing and revising the game as needed, to maximize their intention.)

<u>Variations:</u>

- Nourishment Pods: Participants each have 10 minutes to ask for what would be most supportive from the others in the group (e.g., "Would you tell me what you see as my strengths?" "Can we all lie on our backs and pretend we're looking up at the stars?" "Can I get everyone's advice on something?"). This can be a powerful practice in making requests, as well as a great rest and integration exercise for more intensive workshops.
- A fast and fun variation of this game for a group is called "Would Y'all?" (or "Would You?" for pairs). These variations focus on exercising the muscle of making requests and co-creating with others.

Guru Game

Length: 45–60 minutes
Configuration: Groups of 3 or 4
Related teachings: Dignity and Humility

Where is your personal balance point between dignity and humility? When threatened, are you more prone to posture or collapse? And how can you find more balance between these parts? The Guru Game is designed to explore this central polarity, and can be a clear window into our patterns of collapse and posture. In this game, we invoke both the wisest and humblest versions of ourselves. And while it has the potential to be played as pure entertainment, when taken as a practice, this game is potent.

As discussed in Chapter 1, dignity is our voice, and humility is our ears. Or said another way, dignity is our trust in our own value, and humility our trust in the value of others. And while "guru" in this game doesn't necessarily refer to a spiritual leader, leaders like Gandhi and Mandela can act as perfect models for how both traits can be embodied simultaneously—and for how each of these qualities can serve to further strengthen the other.

Guru Game is especially sensitive to context-setting, so be sure when facilitating that you're clear in your intention. If your intention is to use this game as a sincere investigation (as opposed to just for fun), be sure to remind participants that this is not about "role-playing." Rather, we are being real and authentic, with the intention to get curious about how we undermine our own power, or prevent ourselves from learning. Of course, this is not about beating ourselves up either. Through inquiring into our patterns with curiosity instead of judgment, we can let go of what's not serving us, and put some new options on the relational menu.

Instructions for Playing:

As the Facilitator, Set Context:

This game is about becoming aware of our relationship to humility and dignity, and our patterns of posture and collapse. The more we practice noticing how these states feel in our hearts and bodies, the more we can start to notice how they show up our everyday lives.

- Have participants move into groups, with the first "guru" seated in a chair and their "disciples" seated on the floor.
- When ready, each guru will announce what they are the guru of, and then give a 2 minute "wisdom teaching" on their topic.
- After this two minutes, disciples have three minutes to ask questions (popcorn-style) of their guru.

Guru Instructions

- *You're the pure embodiment of dignity. This doesn't mean you know everything, but that you trust that what you do know has value.*
- *Take a moment to tune in with something that you know deeply, and feel called to share with others. Be sure to pick something that resonates with you, which can be a specific*

topic or a more abstract concept (e.g., compassion, poetry, having fun, or keeping plants alive). Trust that you are the embodiment of this topic.

- *You are welcoming disciples who have traveled from all over the world, to sit at your feet and listen to the wisdom of your words.*

- *You'll start by saying,* "My name is _____ and I am the guru of ___." *Then give a two-minute wisdom teaching on your chosen subject. Try not to worry too much about what you're going to say, and as best you can, just start speaking from the heart. At the end of your talk, invite questions from your disciples.*

- *As you speak, you might notice:*
  - *Is your impulse to go into "posturing" and just trying to look smart?*
  - *Is there an impulse to collapse and doubt that you have anything valuable to say?*
  - *Or are you somewhere in the middle—feeling free to simply be yourself?*

Disciple Instructions

- *You are the pure embodiment of humility.*
- *As your guru is speaking, trust that whatever they have to say has the potential to change your life.*
- *When they are done with their talk, you'll have the opportunity to ask questions. Choose your questions with sincerity, and consider that whatever answer you're given may be exactly what you need to hear.*
- *As you listen, you might notice:*

- *Is your tendency to blindly absorb whatever the guru says?*
- *Do you have an impulse to resist or to harshly question their words?*
- *Or are you somewhere in the middle—curious, attentive and open?*

Complain Game

Length: 30 minutes
Configuration: Pairs
Related Teachings: Own Your Experience, Hologram

It might seem that the Complain Game would be all about complaining. In fact, we use complaining as a gateway to the core practice of *Own Your Experience* (taking full responsibility for our reactions to people and circumstances). One example of what ownership looks like in practical terms is the "I statement". Instead of saying, "You're making me angry," we can say, "Hearing that, I notice I feel angry." This way of speaking is largely derived from Nonviolent Communication, as mentioned in Chapter 3.

Yet there can be a tendency for people to misuse ownership language: to say, for example, "I feel like you're controlling me!" or "I feel like you're not giving me the space I need." Just because you start a sentence with "I feel" doesn't mean it is ownership language! A good indication that it is *not* ownership is if the sentence begins with "I feel like…" or "I feel that…" especially when what follows is not an emotion. Correct ownership language according to NVC would be, "When you told me you didn't want me to see friends, I felt frustrated. My story is that I'm being confined, and I have a need to spend time with other people." A lot of self-awareness and communication skill is needed to come to this point, and NVC is a vital component of the tenets of AR.

At the same time, true ownership goes beyond mere *I feel* statements, and even beyond ownership language in general. It's in our attitudes and our actions, and conveyed through our energy as well as through our language. When we're in full ownership, we become part of the solution to any problem we're facing. To truly own our experience embody the emotional maturity we wish to see in the world.

This is why, paradoxically, sometimes complaining is an access point to ownership. Though it may seem counterintuitive, fully embraced "complaining" can also be a deeply embodied place. And in order to own our experience, we must first get intimate with it. The Complain Game is designed to explore the essence of this teaching.

Thus it begins with welcoming—getting to know our inner "victims" and all the voices of our complaints. These voices are alive in all of us, whether we're consciously acting on them or not. From here, eventually we move to the voices of our "higher selves." This dialogue becomes a bridge, enabling us to become more integrated and whole. Approach this exercise with humility, and you never know what you might harvest.

Instructions for Playing:

As the Facilitator: Set Context:

This is a game all about owning our own experience—through first fully welcoming our complaints. We will play in pairs, and each person will get a chance to play both roles. In each of three rounds, we will move deeper into ownership, eventually into what we call "the integrated adult."

Round 1

- Person A should pick something that's bothering them in their life right now, and for two minutes, allow themselves to fully complain. The topic could be something very specific in their life (i.e., a person or event), or something more broad (i.e., an issue in the world). Whatever they pick, they should be as unrestrained and unfiltered as possible—this is not the time for ownership language!
- Person B should simply listen, and when the time is up, offer a statement of empathy (e.g., *That sounds really tough*).
- Then, Person B can immediately begin complaining about their own situation, from this same approach of non-restraint.

Round 2

- Person A then gets into the voice of their "higher self," whatever that means to them. Person B becomes simply Person A's mirror, so that Person A can "talk to themself," as their higher self. (For example, if Person A is named Jason, they can address Person B: *Jason, this is your higher self. I've heard what you said, and I want to respond.*
- For two minutes, Person A continues, responding to themselves and addressing the original complaint from the perspective of their higher self. Person B simply listens.
- Switch roles and repeat the process.

In between Rounds 2 and 3, facilitators include this teaching (in their own words):

> *So far, we have explored two different perspectives: that of the "complainer" and that of the "higher self." The point here isn't that one of these is right and one is wrong; it isn't that we should be our higher self all the time. In fact, both of these parts provide wisdom and are necessary. And in Round 3 we'll get a chance to combine the two perspectives, as the "integrated adult."*

Round 3

- With Person B again acting as Person A's mirror, Person A can again begin speaking to themselves, this time from the perspective of the "integrated adult." In practical terms, this often looks like the "middle way" between the two voices, and includes tangible next steps. (i.e., What can you realistically commit to doing about this situation, as the person you are today?) Person A will have two minutes to speak from this place, with B just listening.
- Switch roles and repeat.
- After both people have gone, invite a freeform discussion for 3–5 min. Players can share impact with each other at this time.

The Now Game (aka Circling)

Length: 30–90 minutes
Configuration: Two or more
Related Teachings: Presence, Appreciation, and Curiosity; The Five Practices.

The final core game of AR is so potent, it's been turned into an entire modality unto itself! The Now Game, also known as Circling, is a form of "relational meditation" that takes place in the here and now. There are many names for and variations of this practice. T-Groups, Encounter Groups, and humanistic psychology, for example, were very popular in the 1970s, and at the height of the Human Potential Movement, there were over 3000 of these groups operating across the US. Gestalt therapy groups used the phrase, "I and thou, here and now" as an anchor for their group work, in reference to the greatly influential work of Martin Buber.[31] During the Human Potential Movement, a popular phrase was, "Get out of your mind and back into your body."

Clearly, the benefits of being here and now have long been explored in many varied practices. But even though we have known of the benefits of being present, that doesn't make it easy! After all, the human mind is entwined with our nervous system, emotions, and body. So not only is the above statement technically inaccurate (we literally can't "get out of our heads" completely), it can even be used as a judgment of how

---

31   Anderson, Rob, et al. *The Martin Buber-Carl Rogers Dialogue: a New Transcript with Commentary.* State University of New York Press, 1997.

somebody is showing up: that they're thinking "too much," being "too logical," or not in touch with their feelings.

The spirit of Authentic Relating, though, is to welcome ourselves and others exactly as we are—even when we're logical, busy-minded, and "in our heads." In fact, about the worst thing we can do when we are stuck in any experience is to judge ourselves for it. The antidote is actually to just allow the experience to be.

So, how does all of this relate to The Now Game? This game is all about exploring what is present, here and now, when we fully welcome every aspect of our experience. In The Now Game, everything—from that "judgy" voice in our heads, to our deepest fear and desire in the moment—is fair game. When we speak from this place of both presence and acceptance, we give space for all sorts of wonderful things to emerge.

Instructions for Playing:

- Start by sitting in a circle. Take 2–3 minutes to "connect to self," either by sitting quietly, or using the guided meditation from Chapter 4. Then go around the circle, and have each member do a present moment check-in, or share for about 30 seconds what they are noticing in the moment (e.g. emotions, physical sensations, or thoughts). A helpful starter might be, *Being here with you all, I notice...* (see The Noticing Game "All-In" variation from Chapter 5).
- After each person has checked in, as the facilitator, you won't need to *do* much. Simply state the three guidelines and the one rule for the game:

Guidelines:

1) Get curious about yourself and others.

2) Reveal your experience as it is happening right now. Keep the discussion on what is in the room, and not on outside or past events and circumstances.

3) Breathe together and weave together. Include the body, the breath, and the impact we have on each other.

The Rule: Never spend more than 10 seconds talking about something that is not here and now. If we bring in life situations or people that are "outside the room," we only speak the headline.

If this rule is broken, anyone can use the signal for "come back to the here and now." This looks like holding up a palm with five fingers spread, then bringing the fingers together as the palm moves down. This will signal everyone in the group to come to silence, return to their present moment experience, and take a deep breath before resuming.

Note: Some facilitators might want to be more directive and hands-on in guiding the experience for the whole group. This is great, as long as the Five Practices are followed. Remember, a crucial element of our role as facilitators is to model the same authenticity and vulnerability that we ask of the group we're facilitating. In other words, we must be sure not to hide behind our role. After all, there is the potential to learn something profound in any moment—even if you're an experienced AR practitioner Circling with novices.

LIGHT GAMES

Broadly speaking, Authentic Relating games have two main superpowers. The first is for creating community, making friends, and having fun (they are called "games," after all!), and the second is for personal growth and emotional intelligence training. Authentic Relating Games Nights, held regularly in nearly 100 communities worldwide, provide a space for both these aims.

The following "Light Games" are some of the best for creating fun and connection, and also have the benefit of being most accessible. They are easy to play, regardless of your audience's skill and experience level—and easily facilitated in a wide variety of environments, including casual events like family dinners or birthday parties.

Google Game

Length: 10–20 minutes
Configuration: Pairs or breakout groups

The purpose of this game is for groups to get to know each other in a fun, light-hearted way. For those newer to AR, it can be an intriguing taste of the deeper curiosity and novelty inherent to the practice—with a lesser degree of vulnerability and presence required than in many other games. Rather than the relational layer, where we spent much of our time in AR, The Google Game resides largely in the realm of the personal (see the *Three Levels of Communication* from Chapter 5). Try this game at parties or on a first date, to spark some fun and interesting stories.

Instructions for Playing:

- In pairs or small groups, one person begins as the focus of attention—the person who will be "Googled." Others ask questions using the format:

  If I were to Google you and [fill in a word or phrase], *what would I find?* These phrases can be concrete or more abstract (e.g., *"If I were to Google you and* [surfing, international travel, joy, concerts, lizards, the color blue...], *what would I find?*).

- In response, the "Googlee" can share a story, memory, or whatever words or thoughts come up in relation to the search term.

- Group members can also "double click" on anything they want the "Googlee" to say more about.

- After five minutes or so, switch roles (if in pairs), or continue rotating through group members until everyone has gone.

- Optionally, have group members share impact with each other for an additional round.

Hot Seat

Duration: 10–20 minutes
Configuration: 4–20 people

This is a classic "edge-pushing" game that gives us permission to ask "juicier" questions. It's recommended as a game to be played with friends you want to go deeper with—and probably to avoid in professional environments! While Hot Seat can be played purely for entertainment's sake, it's also a potent game for rediscovering our full aliveness—and expanding our willingness to explore more vulnerable topics. Sometimes this means the questions take on a darker or more sexual tone. However, they do not need to.

The pacing of this game contributes to the "edginess" of the experience. Rather than the deep listening that characterizes many AR games, participants are encouraged to fire off questions continuously. This adds to the sense of excitement and playful chaos, creating some degree of pressure for the person "in the hot seat." This is all designed to be in good fun.

Instructions for Playing:
- In groups, one person volunteers to sit in the "hot seat," facing the rest of the group. Set a timer for 3–6 minutes.
- During this time, other participants can ask this person *anything* that they are curious about. Examples:
  - *When was the last time you cried?*
  - *What's a part of yourself that you usually hide from others?*

* *Who in this room are you most sexually attracted to and why?*

Questioners can say "thank you" at any point, to indicate they are satisfied—at which point, the speaker should stop talking and the next question can be asked.

Note: In larger groups (i.e., of 10 or more), a moderator can be useful. In this case, participants raise their hands to ask questions, and the moderator chooses who asks next.

Anybody Else

Duration: Any

Configuration: Groups of five or more

As humans, the importance of "tribe" and group cohesion has been deeply imprinted into our nervous systems over thousands of years of evolution. While, as a species, we've become incredibly diverse, our need for a sense of "togetherness" remains integral. How can we create healthy communities in the face of such deep divides?

For a group to truly know itself, its members must experience both their similarities and differences, in the presence of the whole. Anybody Else seeks to create this experience, through revealing both the uniqueness and the unity of any group of human beings.

This game is one of the most frequently played in AR, for good reason. It's simple to facilitate, and can be both fun and profound for participants. Because of its ability to create coherence in any group, it's a great one for corporate retreats and other workshops with diverse audiences.

Instructions for Playing:

- Arrange participants in a circle (standing or sitting), with some space between each person.
- Set the context. Anyone can then step into the center of the circle and share something that is true about them, followed by the question, *Anybody else?*

- Anyone who has a similar experience or shares this attribute steps into the circle with the speaker.
- Give a moment for everyone to look around and take in this new information about the group, before the next person self-selects to share.

There are many categories of items that might be useful to cover with a group that's new to each other and needs to ease into connection (e.g., age, marital status, children, or country of origin). However, the real magic of Anybody Else is in getting underneath the surface, and exploring our vulnerabilities and the more challenging parts of being human. Often, this leads to a realization that we are not alone. Examples:

I have lost a member of my extended family recently. Anybody else?

I am struggling to find my calling or purpose in the world at this phase in my life. Anybody else?

Anger is an emotion that I am uncomfortable with expressing and feel a lot of shame when I do. Anybody else?

I am new to this group, and feeling intimidated because it seems like a lot of people know each other. Anybody else?

Note: There are many different configurations of this game, including a version where people run and compete for seats, musical chairs style! Anybody Else works very well in online video meetings as well.

SENTENCE STEMS

Sentence Stems are a simple and versatile tool to practice Authentic Relating with groups of any size, and in a wide variety of environments. They are highly effective at building connection between people who are unfamiliar with each other, and just as valuable for close friends seeking deeper intimacy. In fact, they are so commonly used in AR that they form the backbone of many other games.

Simply put, a "sentence stem" is the beginning of a sentence, for which the rest can be uniquely completed by each person in a pair or group. They are used so often because they provide structure and a starting place for people to share, while having a quality of open-ended exploration, allowing people to take things in the direction they want.

One way to use stems is to bring them to a dinner party or family reunion, because it gives people a way to connect without needing to have a background in Authentic Relating. Sentence Stems can also be used to uncover intimate territory between lovers, friends, or any variation of human relationship. The following are some of the most commonly used stems, arranged in different categories of relational investigation. Feel free to explore and write your own custom stems.

Revealing
Something I don't share with everyone is...
Something I am scared to share with you is...
If you really knew me, you would know...
What keeps me up at night is...

When no one is looking, I am...
I open up the most when...
Something I'm not proud of is...
Something I'm really proud of is...

Projection

What I think you think about me is...
A way I want to be seen by others is...
The fish in that fish bowl over there is feeling...
What I do to impress people is...

Expressing Desire

Right now with you/this group, I want...
With you/this group, I imagine...
If this were our last day on earth, the experience I'd like to create with you/this group is...

Communicating Appreciation

What I really get about you is...
The gift I see you bringing to community is...
The values I see you standing for are...
Something I really admire/enjoy/appreciate about you is...

Describing Interactions

My first impression of you was...
Where I felt you the most was...
Something I'm enjoying about being with you is...
Something that's uncomfortable about being with you is...

Outside-the-Box Thinking

I am beginning to suspect...

The truth is...

Right now, it seems obvious that...

The adventure I want to go on with you/this group is...

One of my superpowers is....

INDEX OF TOOLS

ADDITIONAL ACKNOWLEDGMENTS

Firstly, I want to thank my editors, without whom I never could have crafted this book and seen it go out into the community to be a resource for this growing movement. Thank you for your dedication and support; it was truly invaluable! Natalie Grigson, Shaina List, River Langford, and Ellyn Kerr, you all brought such heart and a beautiful eye to this document.

In the beginning of this journey, I named half a dozen people who significantly influenced my thinking and development as an AR practitioner. Readers should know that the movement is truly being led by hundreds of people. Some of the pioneers I would like to thank are: Mark Michael Lewis, Kendra Cunov, Shana James, Lorena Palazzo, Garrison Cohen, John Church, Shay Pausa, Amy Silverman, John Thompson, Jordan Allen, Sean Wilkinson, Michael Blas, Anke Verhees, Mark Boughton, Heather McClellan, Peter Will Benjamin, Susan Campbell, Robbie Carlton, Simon D'Arcy, Michael Welp, Crystallin Dillon, Alison Bulman, Kraye Grymonnt, Guy Sengstock, Melody Markel, Josh Zemel, Rick Smith, Ronja Sebastian, Chad Phillips, Jahmaya Kessler, Jessica Tartaro, and Booster Blake. And, there are so many others. The world has benefited greatly from your authenticity and dedication to supporting others in finding their authentic voice. Also a deep bow and sacred fist bump to my embodiment teachers: Sarah Bryden, Mark Walsh, Amber Ryan, Seth Braun, Zhen Dao, the waters, the air, and mother earth.

There are a few souls who have influenced my journey on this planet far beyond the scope of Authentic Relating. The soulful writing of author A. H. Almaas, and the unique perspective of the Diamond Approach, have been constant guides for me in glimpsing the truth of what it means to be human. The polarity of the human and divine is illuminated through these teachings, and I am eternally opening through this wisdom I have been gifted. To my Diamond Heart teachers, Anne Laney, Andreas Muskos, and especially Gina Crago, thank you for the pearls of guidance you offered me. Also, the Integral Movement, led by philosopher Ken Wilber—and especially the early Integral teachers Diane Hamilton, Terry Patten, Jeff Salzman, and Fred Koffman—influenced the trajectory of my development in formative years when I first arrived in Boulder, Colorado. Truly, I am walking in their footsteps.

ABOUT AUTHENTIC REVOLUTION

Since 2013, Authentic Revolution has been resourcing community builders and training facilitators to spread this practice around the world. Much of the curriculum in this book is distilled from my life experiences and study, including the integration of my study of psychology and mindfulness with the social technology of Authentic Relating.

The mission of Authentic Revolution is to change the world, one connection at a time. We dream of a world where emotional education is common place and the experiences of safety, community, compassion, and generosity are rewarded and acknowledged. We endeavor to reach as many people as possible with these profound connection practices so that we can learn the art of conscious communication and celebrate our differences. The trainings and courses offered through Authentic Revolution are focused on helping people develop embodied authenticity and skillful communication, because we believe that empowering the individual is the best way to affect the collective. We have also trained thousands of leaders to create community through leading authentic relating games nights. AR communities can be found in over 20 countries around the world.

The Authentic Relating Games Manual has been translated into German and Russian and will always be offered as a pay what you can resource. Auth Rev is committed to keep Authentic Relating open-sourced, decentralized and as accessible as possible to all people.

Visit us on the web: www.authrev.com
Or email us: love@authrev.com

ABOUT THE AUTHOR

Equal parts artist, philosopher, teacher, and media producer, Jason is a modern renaissance man. From 2003–2012 he worked for Integral Institute to create thousands of hours of educational media on the topics of transpersonal psychology, spirituality, productivity, and personal growth.

Obsessed with how humans can live and relate optimally, he's facilitated groups and taught authentic relating and circling since 2012. In 2017, Jason co-founded Authentic Relating Training International and has led courses in 20 cities around the world. He lives in Boulder, CO.

Printed in Great Britain
by Amazon

21765761R10137